THESE GOT ME PUNCHED

a book of 50 kisses

NICHOLAS J. STEVENS

www.mascotbooks.com

For more information, please contact:
Mascot Books
620 Herndon Parkway, Suite 320
Herndon, VA 20170
info@mascotbooks.com

Library of Congress Control Number: 2019902750

CPSIA Code: PRV0919A
ISBN-13: 978-1-64307-518-1

Printed in the United States

Dedicated to
Nicholas J. Stevens Sr. (1946—2018)
Thank you, Dad.

Though I know I'll never lose affection
For people and things that went before,
I know I'll often stop and think about them.
In my life, I love you more.

"In My Life," The Beatles
(But I like the Johnny Cash version better.)

I

We were shuffling in a line around a very large circular table. It was topped with flat boxes filled with papers of all shapes and sizes, poundages, and finishes. These papers were the kinds of absorbent, pastel colors they paint doctors' offices and prisons. These papers were meant to welcome and familiarize new students with their new institution of higher learning. These papers would be cast aside and hopefully recycled.

The purpose of this tedious merry-go-round was to assemble packets to be mailed to the parents of incoming freshmen. There had to be at least 500 copies of each page and a mountain of envelopes to feed once we finished collecting and neatly tri-folding right below the line that started with, "Imagine…"

It was mind-numbing to watch the same ass roll along in front of you for nearly an hour while your fingerprints slowly rubbed flat against the paper. It was like a chain gang collecting trash in leg irons, except when the trash was collected, we would mail it out to people who would read and summarize it for their disinterested offspring. Lists of events, names of various old white people, maps, campus bus schedules, some coupons to a car wash or something (freshmen were forbidden to have cars their first year anyway), and information included only to rectify wobbly tables. It was amazing how a body could handle so many of these thin wedges of neatly typed instructions, and never have any idea what any of them said.

We were about halfway through the stack when Stacey got a phone call, and we decided to accept it as a sign we should all stop working. It had rained hard that morning, but you didn't expect it to last, and by the time lunch rolled around (like the ass in front of me), the ground was dry enough to sit on, and only the creases of the streets were still wet.

I was sitting at my desk trying to cut out a cartoon figure from a box of candy to apply to my name tag. I never had a desk of my own in an office setting and so, out of confusion and inexperience, I filled it with candy and office supplies.

I loved pens, and I spent a great deal of time arranging them in rows, first with all the caps on top, then alternating to make them fit closer together. I had a beige phone on the desk with a little red light on it that flickered when it rang. It had a piercing metallic ring to it, so once I figured out the part about the light, I turned off the ringer completely.

It was flickering now, but I waited to answer until I got the last layer of the thicker cardboard off the back of my cutout lemonhead from the candy box. I shared a slab of concrete iced with very thin carpet—a cubicle as they have deemed it in the corporate world—with Stewart and Tim. Stewart told me my phone was ringing, which he felt he needed to do since I turned the ringer off several days before. It flickered its bright red, plastic sputtering, and he told me again. I shot a look of disingenuous thanks as I picked it up and gave him a very smug thumbs-up.

I hated this little game. It was a girl. She sounded very cute, very playful, but I hated this game. I don't dare answer a name at all since I don't know how cute she is yet, and I don't want her to get mad or hang up.

I decided that I didn't really care if whoever it was hung up for being called the wrong name since I was having a hard time being interested in someone who would play around asking, anyway. Cute voice, though. I thought about it, and then started naming names of people I surely didn't know in a hurried attempt to be charming. Margie? I did know a "Margie," but no one would ever believe that. Evelyn? Aunt Faye? Mrs. Carmel?

Ivy. She was cute. She had very light blonde hair cut almost above her ears in the back, then parted with a little wave in the front. She was supposed to be somewhere for the summer that was not near here, and I should have known where it was since I wrote to her at least once, but she had come from there to here and was now downstairs. Maybe I gave her the number when I wrote to her, but I don't think so.

I told Stewart to tell ol' lady Riggings I had gone to do something important, and to give those envelopes hell in my absence. I don't know how real office jobs go, but we didn't punch in or out ever, and we were out often to run errands of all kinds, sometimes with a dolly. Not the Ivy kind of dolly, but the two-wheeled kind. I always felt very focused and purposeful with the dolly and would often take it even when I had no earthly reason to do so.

Ivy was right outside the door downstairs, and for a second, I couldn't see her until my eyes adjusted from the lifeless, crappy fluorescent lighting inside to the bright sun outside. Her hair was even shorter than I remembered, and almost white under the intense glare of the post-rain sunlight. As I approached her, she, in turn, took a few steps towards me and opened her arms to erase any confusion about what kind of greeting ensued.

She had on a striped tank top, and I only noticed as we tightened together and my hands lay flat against her shoulders she was a very well-defined girl. It was as if her skin had been pulled tight over still wet clay that could be shaped with every movement of her body. It was nice and instantly comfortable.

I'm not sure we discussed or so much as mentioned where we were going, but we proceeded to an ice cream shop about six or seven blocks into town. It was a beautiful day by that point, and the reprieve from the rain released a lot of people from their buildings and desks to enjoy it. I was glad to be walking with her, and it added something that everyone else seemed to be in a wink-and-smile mood, too.

The ice cream place was run by some "crunchy" people (like nature folks or hippies or whatever), and they made all the ice cream and cones right there on site. In a brilliant stroke of marketing, or simply from being too hot inside, they left their door open all the time, and you could smell the waffle cones from no less than two blocks in every direction. Anticipation of a good thing is almost better than the thing itself, and we were practically floating on it all the way there.

She opted for cherry vanilla, and I had a new flavor made from Nilla Wafer cookies. It was probably the best ice cream I had ever had, but I was enamored by the fact that even after trying mine and agreeing, she had no regrets about hers. There is also something to be said about a girl who doesn't ask you to trade because yours is better and who doesn't make you feel bad for enjoying it yourself.

They must have forgotten to put their signature piece of candy in the bottom of her cone because it was leaking like crazy all over her hand. She was quite tan and had bright green nail polish on her short nails that had started to chip off all but her thumb. The combination of this and the melting ice cream made for a palate I thought would have been a nice photograph.

We had forgotten napkins and were a mess when we stopped on a hill at the park nearby. The slanted field of the hill faced the sun and was spotted with readers, dogs, and couples trying to wipe off ice cream onto the lush grass. It was useless, but she offered up a bottle of water from her backpack to rinse at least our hands.

I was vainly trying to reach a dried droplet of Nilla Wafer ice cream on my chin with my outstretched tongue when, in mid-laughter, she leaned over and put her mouth on mine. I reached over and felt the side of her body, and half-fell back onto my elbow. Her kiss was very much like the hug we shared earlier that afternoon; I was wrapped in it completely. She leaned back and smiled, and I must have looked ridiculous with awe because she began laughing, and not with the polite laughter of conversation, but of true pleasure of the moment. It was a quick spout of amusement, and she made no apologies for finding humor in my bewilderment.

Then, just as suddenly, she got up, and motioned back to the city.

In front of the building was a very wide, two-lane road striped with parking lines on both sides. The road lay between the student union and a massive gothic cathedral that had been turned into lecture halls and classrooms. Coincidentally, automobiles and the people traveling in them were accustomed to dodging pedestrians and careless students passing back and forth between the two.

Her friends were already patiently waiting near the entrance of the building near a frozen ice stand that I never noticed until now. We stopped at the edge of one of the parking spots, and we mutually leaned in for another embrace and to press our lips together before departing. Not being taken by surprise this time, I was able to realize the beauty and warmth of her slightly open mouth. It must have been longer than I thought because I winced when I opened my eyes, and they were struck by the glare of that bright sun. She held my hand for an extra moment, and then released it as I paused to turn and say goodbye once again.

II

I filled a paper cup with the hottest water I could find, which in this case was from the three-head espresso machine on the wall to my right. It was a slow day, but through the massive wall of glass that made up the front of the store you could see a lot of bodies moving about on the street, marred only by the static of falling leaves. The sidewalk was our own personal aquarium and you could do almost anything and the people outside (or inside, depending on how you looked at it) seemed to have no idea. They did notice, however, if you tapped on it as they walked by.

The water was for my comb, which was coated with pomade and a layer of lint that had caked on it. Melting everything off it was really the only way to get it completely clean, and as long you kept it away from the other cups, so no one would try to drink it, it sat long enough to do so. Some of my co-workers thought it was too disgusting to leave around, and I found myself repeatedly explaining how truly gross it would have been to have lint pulled through the arcing mound of hair neatly coiffed upon my head.

Bear went down to the noodle place to get lunch and had become just another plastic diver man as he bobbed heavily down the street. He laughed at me often, but almost never seemed to be in a good mood or content with anything at all. I always felt a little uncomfortable around him but liked him very much and tried my best to get him to brighten up, even if only for an instant.

Sometimes this meant mimicking his malaise to relate, and joining in the bitter, cynical, and yet usually humorous observations about things. I had grown warm inside once when he affectionately referred to me as his "disco ball of hate" since I accepted his intense, concentrated hatred of everything and everyone and evenly distributed it in many other directions. I was glad to have his acceptance in some form or another, though the moniker didn't really suit me.

As my vista followed him bumping past the neatly dressed museum types and students he loathed so much, I was taken aback by a splendid creature sliding down towards our doorway. She first tried the smaller glass door that led into the sitting area, but of course found it locked. We never used it and even if it had been unlocked, there was a table and a rather dumpy, goateed grad student parked in front of it. This only supported my belief about no one being able to see in.

She quickly released the handle and inconspicuously looked over her shoulder to see if anyone had seen her make the grievous error of not being familiar with the establishment and its entrances. She did not notice that I had been staring at her the whole time through the biscotti jar and smiling both out of adoration and humor at her expense.

She stood very far away from the counter and appeared to be looking more over the menu board above me and onto the balcony that made up the second floor. She finally decided on what would have been her usual if she had ever been there before and proceeded to take a very forced air of disinterest while she ordered it. I, in turn, was forcing charm while stirring the hot water with my comb and blowing on it, hoping to provoke a reaction and a subsequent conversation.

She took the farthest possible seat along the long wall of the sitting area and just sat looking up at the paintings that whoever we were giving free space to that month had so generously hung. After a minute or so, Bear came back with his noodles and a complaint about something, and I directed his attention to my new subject of interest. He begrudgingly agreed that she was, in fact, pretty and, being annoyed by my boyishly nervous hesitation, ordered me to either go talk to her or just stop talking altogether.

I grabbed a filthy rag and headed out into the open room to clean all the tables around hers. It took a good four tables, about 10 chairs, and a very stubborn ring of dried mocha before she looked over and smiled. I smiled back in the way you take a compliment you think someone is making just to be polite. It turned out it was genuine, and I leaned onto the chair opposite her to begin the interrogation.

Her name was Eden, which she claimed was Egyptian. There are many myths about the old world I don't buy into, but the beauty of an Egyptian girl is one that I firmly believe in (I knew one other previously and their shared splendor was enough proof for me).

Since she appeared to be doing absolutely nothing anyway, she agreed to walk up to the shops on Walnut Street at the conclusion of my shift, which ended with the last of Bear's upon. I calmly and quickly walked back behind the counter and stood over Bear while bouncing on my toes and repeatedly asking him if he was done yet. He was much larger than I and the dangling bent metal of the first aid cabinet clinging to the wall was proof of his temper, as was the hole in the drywall behind it, but I felt fairly certain I would be granted amnesty on the grounds of romance. He grunted a "go!" and crumpled up the sad remains of his overcooked noodles, and I wrestled with whether to tell him about the slash of soy sauce that had somehow gotten next to his earlobe. I opted not to; I was in kind of a hurry.

She met me in front of the counter and promptly ignored the offer of my extended elbow as we walked out amongst the rest of the life aquatic. She had on a light blue, short-sleeved angora sweater and matching eye shadow over her haunting, sleepy eyes. I looked around while she spoke to make sure as many other people as possible could see I was walking with her, but no one seemed to notice except a man selling those street flowers that died when you unwrapped them from their cellophane. I didn't buy any and I was glad she was ignoring him too.

We arrived at my apartment, which was on the way to Walnut Street, and she asked if I wanted to change clothes before continuing. I made a joke about never changing just to please her and her profound indifference was leading me to believe she was either hard of hearing or completely and utterly humorless. I longed for the tender ear of gristly ol' Bear.

From the other room, I could hear her ask if she could put on music, and I told her to put on (or take off) whatever in the world she wanted. This, too, went right by her and she began to call out names of artists, not quite loudly enough to imply she wanted approval, but just as if she were cataloguing them in her head.

Despite changing clothes, I still smelled an awful lot like coffee, but she seemed to like coffee so I hoped it would work in my favor. I had a clean comb at home and took an extra second to reshape my hair and pull down one or two strands that were supposed to look accidental. I could hear her singing along in the other room, and I wouldn't have noticed if I hadn't already been looking in a mirror, but the sound of it pulled up my nose into a crinkled, unappealing expression I had to forcefully smooth out before rejoining her.

I sat close on the couch and began asking her all kinds of questions about family, work, school, and whatever else I thought might spark some interest in her as more than a bright blue angora sweater. She was daintily pulling at my fingers as I spoke and then I abruptly kissed her mid-sentence. It was rhythmic and far more fervent than I had expected. It lasted for quite some time, all the while she kept repositioning herself, so my hands found as much of the sweater as possible.

I had an affinity for sweaters with nothing but the unmentionable worn underneath. I liked how the soft fabric met the skin and it made me want to be in between them. It was forbidden on my only attempt and I had no intention of pressing the issue since the verdict was still out on her overall, though the jury was leaning towards a mistrial.

When we broke, the conversation took a less question-and-answer tone and turned to matters of relationships. She asked about girlfriends, and it was revealed I had kissed more girls than I had dated, a fact that seemed to be fairly common and entirely reasonable. She had not. Not girls, I mean, but never kissed anyone she had not dated or eventually dated. In awe, I asked again, and she repeated her answer. In awe, I asked again. This time her response was, "Well, we'll see tomorrow."

I waited a little longer on the couch and against that sweater and the skin underneath to end the suspense, but she had now.

III

Drew and I had been stranded at the mall earlier that evening when we missed the last available bus back to campus, due to our own poor judgment and a bad tip we got from another bus driver.

After a series of misfortunes, random occurrences, and one act of suspicious kindness from a man who both smoked a comically large pipe and held a conversation without moving his lips, we made it back to campus to regale our tale to our band of merry friends.

They were already well into the 40-ounce bottles of cheer they commissioned a homeless man to get for them. It was the quiet guy with the dreadlocks and beard we had previously coached to be more assertive in his attempts to subsidize his needs, in whatever form they presently took. Before then, he barely spoke above a whisper and, if questioned, he rarely repeated his request for fear that you were starting trouble with him. You still had to post a lookout at each entrance of the store, so he wouldn't just take the money—or the malt beverages—and split. His lack of gratitude was disconcerting.

Quite a crowd had gathered around the stone bench we confiscated for our stage once we broke into our unrehearsed routine of thrashing physical gestures and free-flowing expletives. We were tagging each other out mid-story to add whatever details the other had let rage momentarily erase from their memory. It was quite a show and despite later attempts, could never be recreated with the same intensity.

Nicholas J. Stevens

The theory that by expelling all our anger and frustration outwardly through story would somehow be therapeutic was pure bunk. I feel comfortable speaking for Drew by saying that we were even worse off than before. Blood raced, veins swelled, jaws clenched, and knuckles whitened with every shouted word. One would expect to feel completely spent after such an eruption, but it was not so.

Neither of us had eaten since the crappy chain restaurant outside the mall where we saw the last bus, our bus, pause momentarily and then lurch forth on its way. That was quite some time ago and we were starving. I felt like running down an animal and tearing a slab of still convulsing meat from its warm hide but settled for the sub place down the street instead.

The thing about anger is that it is absolutely contagious, especially in an urban setting and especially at night. During the two-block walk, Drew had received no less than two threatening glares and I had been unsuspectingly spun by a stout shoulder thrust into me by some nondescript auditioning tough guy. Brody, who we picked up after the performance, was not noticeably angry about anything. He had, to this point, been left alone entirely, but that, too, would change.

There was quite a line in the sub place and the wait caused by their normal leisurely pace was only compounded by some sort of altercation between one of the only female housing impaired ladies in town and the unfortunate individual who was stamped as that night's manager. On a normal evening, I would have enjoyed the tête-à-tête between the two—hers covered with what could best be described as "English teacher hair" and his hidden behind what was quite possibly the largest mustache I had ever seen. But, none of us were in the speaking mood and, considering the dense mound of shit we had already dredged through in the last five or so hours, we thought it better to just order and leave without any further problems.

I hadn't even noticed that it happened, but apparently one of the half dozen frat boys in front of us (who I normally only consider background scenery on a college campus, aside from the occasional death by alcohol poisoning or sexual assault) had made a hissing sound in our general direction. Brody looked, pulled a confused face, and then looked away.

We opted to wait no longer, and wouldn't you know it, but not four steps outside of the shop we were turned by a loud "hey!" It was the largest of the six, wide at the shoulders and clad in a turtleneck sweater, jeans, and one of those braided leather belts that flips over itself and hangs down in a proud, phallic gesture. I disliked him already.

They closed all but a foot or two of the distance between us and began demanding an apology from Brody for looking at them a few minutes earlier. Apparently, they were aiming for the attention of a young woman by hissing and got Brody instead. Brody was tall, but rail thin and easily earmarked as the weakest of the three of us. Drew was only slightly taller and lean, but had good musculature, and as I knew from wrestling with him around our room, was quite strong and never willing to submit under any pressure or bodily harm.

For reasons I will never fully understand, Drew, seizing the role of mediator, did so in the lowest gravel of a voice he could muster—a voice that was octaves away from his own. Until this point, blood raced, veins swelled, jaws clenched, knuckles whitened, et cetera, but now, a turned brow quickly turned into a half-turned brow and I was just confused—still angry, but really confused. He sounded like he should be taking requests from the crowd at some smoke-filled jazz club instead of defending our friend against the ill-directed accusations of this band of beer-filled troglodytes. I still just wanted to swing, and I would have probably been beaten senseless that night and been the target of every clone in their organization for the remainder of my years at school, but I didn't care.

In an even more confusing and much more disappointing move, Brody apologized. For what he did not know and why he could not say, but he said he was sorry. You could tell that they, too, were disappointed they would have to put their collective heads together to devise another method of inciting violence from someone else. I just shook my head and averted my eyes from his general direction. I suppose it was all part of the universe balancing itself out because Drew and I had grown exponentially stronger friends over the course of our ordeal and never, at any point, turned on each other or assigned blame in any way. But I lost a great deal of respect for another good friend after that uttered apology. I shook my head again and started back to the dorm, no longer lending thought to the hunger that was still unfed.

I just wanted to go to sleep. I was certain I would have difficulty doing so since I depleted no energy fighting or being beaten or whatever. Waves of anger, now combined with hurt, resentment, more frustration, and the newly remembered appetite were not going to fare well on a pillow. My dorm was very far up a hill and I had been staying with an acquaintance in her room often, at least on the weekends. She was prone to blinding drunkenness and was nowhere to be found. I had long ago run out of patience, but I knew that if I did wait, she would arrive before too long.

Then I saw Cindy. She was a bigger girl who was a principal in our circle of friends and whose abrasive attitude (and size) often prompted our ridicule and torment. Drew had, on numerous occasions, preemptively introduced her presence in the cafeteria by thumping the bottom of our table to make circular ripples in my water glass, like in that dinosaur movie. She would arrive seconds later amidst our uncontrollable laughter and become instantly enraged, assuming we were laughing at her...which we were.

She was a pretty girl with a pleasant, round face but fierce eyes. When she was smiling, she looked conniving and when she wasn't, she looked just plain mean. Most of the initial torment was a result of a slight, but unsure crush I had on her. I knew my hesitation irritated her and I don't think she was all that stable to begin with.

We had kissed once on our way out of my dorm room when everyone had met there one evening to attend a party on the hill. We were the last two out of the room, by my design, and I grabbed her and kissed her very passionately before smiling and walking out the door, never to mention it again. I didn't necessarily regret it but had no intention of pursuing it and then it just got ugly.

Following the incident in my room and several attempts by her to make sense of my actions, she made her feelings towards me very clear and they were not of a positive nature. I had seen her out huffing furniture polish from the front pocket of a pair of bib overalls and we...well, she made quite a public spectacle. Tonight, I expected nothing less than a complete meltdown.

She was on acid and already crazy and I could see her making a beeline towards me from across the stone thoroughfare. There was no avoiding it and I could hear the quickening kettle drum in my head as she split the crowd in half. In a flash of glass and spittle, she drenched me with an artificially-flavored fruit beverage and a flurry of obscenities.

I stood frozen in ire, soaked to my skin and even now starting to stick to myself. Then, in keeping with the theme of the rest of the evening, something unexpected happened. I was fine. I was on a beach in the sun or in a field being licked by tall grass or whatever scenario that beverage company would have loved as

Nicholas J. Stevens

their advertisement. It was as if every negative, awful, horrible feeling that pumped through me was washed away by a wave of kiwi strawberry.

Someone pulled her away, I found another stone bench, sat down, and just closed my eyes until I heard Symon's sweet slur inviting me upstairs.

IV

Since it fell on a day of the week when the sun was expected to rise, I had to work on my 20th birthday. I would be free by mid-afternoon and I liked work just fine, so I didn't really mind. Also, I was expecting to get gifts from everyone I knew and there was no chance I would go in if I didn't have to work, so it was a good opportunity to receive bountiful offerings from those I knew for certain had paying jobs.

Chris, my fellow manager, was not really a good guy. He was a charming guy the way Ted Bundy probably was, and everyone liked him, but he was not necessarily a good guy. He smiled big most of the time and some of the rapidly approaching-middle-age women that worked at the hospital across the street liked him a whole lot and would occasionally give him oral sex in the office down the hall from where we kept the milk. That could have played a part in why he smiled so big all the time, but it was unnerving and devious, nonetheless.

He liked me a good deal and we hung out outside of work on a few occasions, mountain biking mostly, but I would not have called him a friend unless he was the one who asked. He was a contradiction, as most people are, and despite his dereliction of duty at work, he was generous with all and seemingly concerned about people in general.

Once, coming back from a biking expedition in the park near the cemetery, he had unexpectedly sliced through four lanes of traffic to wedge himself in between two teenagers and an elderly Asian man on one of those old beach cruiser bicycles with the

Nicholas J. Stevens

basket on the front. The teenagers had formed a two-man barricade across the narrow sidewalk and were trying to convince the man to let them "borrow" his bike. He was shaking his head and trying to cover up his underlying fear by pretending to not really understand what they were saying. By the time I finally made my way through traffic, Chris had thrown down his bike and was in a fighting stance in front of the bigger of the two teenagers.

Chris was shorter and stocky, with a belly that was in transition from pooch to gut, but you could see as he held his forearms perpendicular to the ground that he was in pretty good shape at one point in his life. Something wise was leaking out of the kid's mouth when he was interrupted by the fingerless-gloved fist attached to Chris's thick forearm. It didn't look as if he had connected with him and I was surprised by the kid's unnatural lack of astonishment when he yanked back his head. His face was just bent in the angry, disillusioned sneer of adolescence when a ribbon of scarlet unraveled from his nostril. He wiped it off on his sleeve, uttered a quick threat, and then turned and left. Chris turned his attention back to the man, who was nodding profusely and thanking him before remounting and starting to pedal in the direction of the two boys. When we stopped him, he pointed and explained that he lived that way. We finally convinced him to take another route home.

When I left work, I did so with a handful of cards that I should have thrown out in the trash can on the corner of the adjacent block (I saved those kinds of things forever for a reason I didn't know) and a very large, bright blue bottle of gin that Chris had given me. It looked like an expensive lamp without the bulb or shade on top and I remember thinking that it would have taken me at least half a decade to consume it in its entirety. I only started drinking on Valentine's Day of that year and although I swore that I had been genetically consecrated with a high tolerance for alcohol, it didn't take much to set me rambling my fool head off.

It was an unspoiled May day and there was a competition between the gleaming bottle in my arm and my face as to which beamed brighter. I thought it would have been next to impossible to shadow my utter contentment, but then I saw the one person who was effortlessly brighter than any bottle or birthday boy.

Evangeline.

She was a good friend of mine since I had started school and had been since I left it. Not the kind of good friend that you call all the time or bring along to make the mundane chores of everyday life more tolerable, though she would have, but she was the kind of friend that you are always halfway into a conversation with. You could skip the banality of "how are you" and "how have you been" since you were pretty okay to be with her anyway.

She was tall and lean and had long, black hair that curled in loops on its own. She was the kind of beautiful that crept up on you in that you knew that she was pretty from far away and even up close, but the more you looked at her, the more she took away your ability to speak or form cognitive thoughts. She was devilishly charming without trying and when she pulled in her bottom lip and the dent in her elfin chin popped in, you couldn't help but be smitten.

I was walking back from stealing some books and a magazine from the campus bookstore one afternoon when I was startled by the loud crack of wet foam on the pavement next to me. Perplexed, I looked up to see Evangeline casting a frothy grin at me and waving a toothbrush back and forth in the air. Not many people could make such audacious horseplay beguiling, but she was not most people.

We met with a hug and she noticed the rather obvious signs that I was celebrating something and, without hesitation, invited me over and requested permission to cook for me on this joyous occasion. Idelle and I had been apart for several weeks and our amicable separation led to her offer to take me out to dinner for my birthday, but that was later. There were no expectations there and I had no better plans for lunch...actually, I had a hard time conceiving of better plans for lunch, so I agreed wholeheartedly.

Her apartment suited her well and was itself very representative of her. I was comfortable immediately and became more taken in as my eyes listened to the details narrated by this picture frame or that piece of clothing draped over that little table and so on. It smelled heavenly, too, even before she put a pan to flame and ignited the kitchen with the orchestral sounds and aroma of apt cooking.

She was amazing.

It didn't take long for my fascination in her (and the meal) to draw me to her back to take in all that I could. I put my hands on either side of her and leaned against the subtle warmth of the hot metal stove. I let go as the heat surged through my hands, and I slid them around her sides, my forearms pressed flat to her stomach as I pulled her against me. With my head on her shoulder and cheek against hers, she let her eyes fall shut for a slow moment. She turned and stepped us away from the stove as she leaned in and kissed me. When she withdrew, she pulled in her lip and directed me to go sit down until she was done.

I swayed back over to the couch and watched her cook the rest of my birthday meal through the wavy aqua glass.

V

An enormous sedan inches up to the corner where a hip Tex-Mex restaurant sits. There are apartments in the former offices above it.

ME: Nice car.

DONNA: Yeah, thanks. It's my mom's.

ME: Really? You don't roll in a 1978 Cutlass? It's not yours?

DONNA: Funny. You could walk, or we could take your ca... Oh, that's right.

ME: Yeah, you're pretty funny yourself. Where are we headed tonight?

DONNA: I thought maybe miniature golf. Is that okay with you?

ME: Well, it's fine by me, but I am not going to let you win just because you're a girl or because you are a girl in a skirt, or because you are a girl in skirt who is all made up. I feel kind of bad. I'm a slob next to you. You look good tonight.

DONNA: Thank you. Was that a "yes?"

ME: Oh, about the golf? Yes, sure. Where is it, by the way?

DONNA: Why? Do you have a favorite?

ME: Well, I used to play "The Skins Game" with Brad and Stewart and some other twits we know, out at the one in Murrysville. It's a nice course. They don't have all the clowns and windmills and shit, it's just a nice course with little sand traps and gravel pits and rock formations and stuff.

DONNA: "The Skins Game?" Sounds a little gay.

ME: No. It's a way of betting. The pros do it. It's like that.

DONNA: I'll bet Stewart loved "The Skins Game."

ME: That's not nice. The old guy that works there, "Fuzzy" his tag read (though I suspect that he's lying), said that there were no straight shots on the whole course. Really something.

DONNA: Good thing for Stewart.

ME: Now you're just being mean, but at least it's not at me.

They have dollar night there a few times each summer where all games of mini golf, bowling, various deals at the snack bar, and whatever else is only a dollar. We didn't take full advantage of it this year, but there's always next year.

DONNA: I think I changed my mind; you're a little too into it.

ME: I'll carjack you and force you to go.

DONNA: You might get me there, but as soon as they give me a club, I'm going to hit you across the neck and run away.

ME: I don't like the way you said that. You've been thinking about it.

DONNA: Just stay in line and you won't have to worry about it.

ME: I plan to, don't worry.

DONNA: Well, you don't have to stay too much in line.

ME: Where did you say it was?

DONNA: I didn't. You started rambling on about dollar night and Fluffy the caddy or whatever.

ME: Fuzzy, and if he's there I am telling him what you said.

DONNA: It isn't that one anyway, it's the putt-putt in Monroeville.

ME: Never heard of it; sounds made up.

DONNA: How's your girlfriend, the one in Florida?

ME: She's not...in Florida, I mean...or my girlfriend. She's not either. Well, she might be in Florida now, I'm not really sure. We haven't spoken since she brought me flowers at work.

DONNA: What?

ME: She brought me flowers to work when I was working.

DONNA: She brought you flowers? What kind?

ME: Yeah, I don't really want to talk about it. It's weird.

DONNA: What kind?

ME: We were already not together, and she thought something or whatever. Yeah, I really don't want to talk about it.

DONNA: What, like roses? She brought you roses?

ME: Yeah, I don't really want to talk about it.

DONNA: But you're a guy.

ME: Yes, thank you. I'm glad we cleared that up. I really don't want to talk about it. Can't we...anything? What about your boyfriend?

DONNA: Who? I don't have a boyfriend.

ME: That guy. You know.

DONNA: No, I haven't had a boyfriend in forever. Who do you mean?

ME: I am completely talking out of my ass, I just wanted to stop talking about my girlfriend bringing me flowers.

DONNA: You mean ex-girlfriend?

ME: Yeah, that.

DONNA: I'm holding off for now anyway, until I can get that someone special.

ME: You mean like the Olympics. Where are we?

DONNA: I have someone in mind.

ME: Where are we?

DONNA: I want to show you something.

ME: Oh? Where is it?

DONNA: Right here. Am I clear in the back? (She focuses intently on the rear-view mirror.)

ME: I don't know what the hell you're talking about, really.

DONNA: Jackass, in the back. Am I going to hit that car?

ME: Probably. You won't do any damage to this thing, though. I can tell you that.

DONNA: That's fine, don't you think? I won't get a ticket, will I?

ME: This car is so big, when we got in, we were already here.

DONNA: You're funny. C'mon.

ME: Are we going to buy crack? Because I was saving it for later, but if we can skip the field trip to the crack house here, I can break it out right now.

DONNA: This is a nice place. You're a jerk.

ME: I'm kidding. Where are we?

DONNA: I used to live here. I want to show you something.

ME: But if you used to live here and you don't anymore, how are we going to get in?

DONNA: Watch. (She manipulates the locks and the door pops open.)

ME: Oh, that's nifty.

DONNA: It's sort of one of the reasons I moved: no security.

ME: Well, that's a shame. If I knew that and you still lived here, there could be trouble.

DONNA: You don't have to break in.

(They ascend the fire escape to the rooftop.)

ME: Say, what's up here? Are you going to push me off?

DONNA: Maybe. It depends.

ME: On what? What the hell did I do?

DONNA: Nothing at all. Absolutely nothing.

ME: This is nice up here. I take back the crack house comment. (He begins meandering around the edge of the roof.)

DONNA: Have a seat, handsome.

ME: This is really something. You can see everything.

DONNA: Yeah, I know. Have a seat.

ME: What is that over there? Is that the...what is it? The building with all the flowers?

DONNA: The conservatory?

ME: Yeah, with the butterflies?

DONNA: They don't have butterflies there all the time. Have a seat.

ME (ignoring her requests to be seated): What do they do with them then? Let them out in the cold? They'd die.

DONNA: Will you sit down, please?

ME (sits down next to DONNA): Oh, yeah. Sorry, I was taken aback. This is really something.

DONNA: Just look at it as one big view, not just individual buildings and things.

ME: It's something.

DONNA: See, the trees on either side of the building frame fit just right so that it's a perfect background.

ME: Yeah. I like the edge where the building, this building, meets the sky. It's a collision of worlds.

DONNA: Do you still want to play mini golf?

ME: No, I'm good. You've done a marvelous job hosting the evening so far. Whatever you want is fine.

DONNA: Is it?

ME: Well, except that pushing me off the edge thing. I'm probably not down with that...pun intended.

DONNA: You are very funny.

ME: Thanks, you're a plum. (pauses and looks around) Boy, it really is something. I can't get over it.

DONNA: What are you thinking about right now?

ME: Right now?

DONNA: Yes. What are you thinking about?

ME: Well, now I'm thinking about the question of what I'm thinking about.

DONNA: But what are you thinking about besides the question?

ME: Oh. The edge. I was thinking about that edge. I have a crazy urge to run over and off of it right into nothing. It's very strong, too. I want to run as fast as I can over to that edge, where that sky meets our ground, and hurl myself off of it. Not in a crazy way, just right off into nothing.

DONNA: I was thinking about kissing you.
ME: Oh. I was thinking about jumping off.
(They kiss.)
ME: Oh.

VI

The backside of the school that faced the parking lot was much less impressive than the grand entrance in the front, which was not impressive at all. The brick was a sandy cream color and the sidewalk was spidered with cracks on every square. I paused there for a second on the stairs while Krista went over to her mom's burgundy Ford LTD to ask if she could give me a ride home.

Smoke and the bag of fat hanging from her mom's arm poured out of the window when she rolled it down to answer her. She looked annoyed, as if someone was making too much noise in the kitchen during "her stories." I glanced back over my shoulder through the cloudy chicken wire window into the hallway to see if anyone else I knew could either give me a ride or walk home with me instead. No such luck.

It was a warm, sunny day and it would be a nice walk until probably near the bingo hall when I predicted I would finally break a sweat. I contemplated going back inside to drop off a book or two that I could get away with not taking home. This would lighten the load and maybe put off dampening my shirt for a few blocks farther past the bingo hall, but I took too long deciding which homework I was going to sacrifice, and Krista motioned me over.

I had apparently been in the same grade with her for both years of high school,but didn't become aware of her until about two weeks ago when she asked me to a dance and I agreed. I guess we had always been in the same grade, except prior to fourth grade when I moved up in the middle of the year. I went to the first half of fourth grade and the last half of fifth when they couldn't give me any more busywork to keep me from causing problems and making fun of those not as intellectually gifted.

Fifth grade was a misleading representation of the rest of my educational career because everyone went out of their way to be nice and make me feel welcome. Plus, I was still right next door to my old friends in the fourth grade if I ever wanted to reminisce.

I don't really know what changed, but sixth grade was a drastic contrast from any classroom setting I had been in up until that point. I was no longer the cool, funny kid I still thought I was and even though it didn't really seem like anything changed about me, how I was treated sure did. Even my other friends were sort of forgetting to invite me to do things since we didn't see each other as much and had recess at different times.

My science fair project, a cross-section model of the layers of earth and the natural resources that lie beneath, made of different colored layers of hobby sand, was shaken up like the clearing of an Etch A Sketch. It was rendered colorful, but meaningless by one of the kids who chased me home earlier that year. I was chased home a few times that year.

That's all I could think about while I was standing waiting to meet the mother of a girl I didn't really know and wasn't really sure I liked enough to iron or wear a tie for. I think she was even friends with one of the kids that grabbed my Puma gym bag and made a dog pee on it back during the days of my torment. Well, he didn't make the dog pee on it—he wasn't magic. He just threw it under the dog as it was peeing. It's strange what the mind will revert to when it isn't interested in what is currently going on or doesn't want to think about it.

The thick paint of the stair railing had gotten soft under the hot sun and my hand stuck momentarily as I released my grip and started towards what I guess was now my ride. A few flecks of the paint stuck to my palm and I just then noticed that the stairs and railing were the same color as that massive box of a car. I conspired in my head to wipe off my hand on the seats, which I imagined were a coarse, durable fabric of the same shade.

She grabbed my arm when I got to the car and introduced me to her mother as we climbed in. Her mom cast back her pleasure to meet me off the rear view mirror like a cab driver. She was much more pleasant than I expected and seemed almost more excited than her daughter, who had transferred her grasp from my elbow to my shoulder and thigh, simultaneously.

I wasn't very experienced with girls and not used to being in such close quarters, so it suddenly became very uncomfortable to sit there. I had my books balanced on my other leg and was trying to hold them in place with my forearm while I held on to the top of her hand. I knew she couldn't, but I kept thinking that her mom could see and would care, which she wouldn't, and I was shifting like mad to find a comfortable position.

It was like the lounge of a bad hotel in the car, everything was covered in dark red velvet and it was thick with the flat stench of stale cigarette smoke. The window in the back was open about an inch and I kept turning my head away from Krista and tilting my neck to get fresh air. She didn't seem to notice and while I was turned, had procured a cigarette from the long rectangular pack in her mother's stout, inverted hand. I don't think I knew that she smoked and if I had, I doubt I would have agreed to be her date to the dance we were set to attend a few nights from now. I felt like I was making a face and I think the muscles underneath the skin on my face were, but she just looked over and smiled a cockeyed smile while blowing a stream of white smoke out of the open corner of her mouth.

I felt a growing dent deep in my stomach and despite the wrenching sickness, I still had the initial problem of balancing

Nicholas J. Stevens

my books to contend with, though that was fading. The breathable air was shrinking rapidly around me and finally her mom must have noticed—though I am probably giving her powers of perception too much credit—and asked if I wanted the window rolled down more.

She didn't wait for a reply and the now fully open outlet granted me amnesty from the smothering cloud that had been slowly extinguishing my breath. I began to worry about my clothes and how desperately I would want to change when I got home. I didn't live that far, but it didn't take long for the stench to saturate both the cloth and skin I was wearing. I was crawling inside my organic and inorganic casings, all the while trying to be pleasant, answer questions, and respond appropriately to the mundane details of her mom's daily existence. Occasionally Krista would cut in and point out that I wasn't interested in hearing about the "Indian guy" at her work or what happened at bowling last night or whatever, an accusation which was entirely accurate but that I emphatically denied.

My mother wouldn't arrive home for another hour and a half at least and my father pulled in at precisely 11:17 p.m. every night. Because of this, we kept a spare key dangling off a nail on the underside of the deck that led to our second floor. I was instructed to keep the key a secret, so if I was dropped off by someone suspect or that I didn't know too well, I would embark on a routine of pretending to look for a key in my bag until they drove away. If they were the type to insist on seeing me actually enter the house, I would simulate opening the door with a pen or foil-wrapped stick of gum—anything shiny—while waving and smiling until they disappeared from sight. I even once faked having to get the mail from the box all the way on the other side of the house just to appease an acquaintance's parents who were overly concerned for my safety. I quickly realized they weren't concerned enough to wait while I lollygagged the length of the side yard.

I was sure that this was one of those times that would require a command performance as I got the impression that although she had no problem with her child smoking during her formative years, she would be quite unrelenting about seeing me in all right.

Ours was an odd driveway and I was gripping the door handle by the time she swung around the luxury American automobile, so she could pull forward onto the busy street. I got out onto the stodgy gravel and Krista got out beside me and put her arms around my neck. I could feel her crisp, product-coated curls fall over my arms as she leaned in and kissed me. She tasted awful.

Without letting our lips become familiar, she formed a small circle with her mouth and slid the firm point of her tongue into my mouth. I accidentally started to inhale and almost choked on her stale breath and the tiny funnel of meat that was moving back and forth in my barely open mouth. She broke away and smiled and I said a polite goodbye and thanks to the section of face in the mirror on the door. As she went around to the passenger's side and got in, I began to fumble in my pocket for the key that wasn't there.

Nicholas J. Stevens

VII

It was Sunday night on the porch. There were only a few drained voices slapping against the hard-concrete walls while most were just bodies standing around smoking and trying to let their studying sift in. It was just after 11:00 p.m. and Brody and I had made the decision that we were done with words and black and white print and highlighters and blue-lined notebooks until our respective alarms went off the next morning.

We had a ritual to attend to as we had every Sunday evening for months now. Pizza and breadsticks would be ordered, and it was my turn to pay, so I would insist to the apron-clad drone on the other end of the phone that I had a coupon for a free order of breadsticks with a purchase of a medium pie or greater, which I did not. The drivers never asked for the coupon and it used to always work until they started to wise up and began asking you very specific questions about the origin of the coupon (some frat boys were selling them) and what it looked like (like a coupon for free breadsticks) and what code was on it (I'm not James Bond, buddy, just don't forget the red sauce...and you can keep that cheese sauce, that shit is toxic). I had a friend who would linger down in the quad next to the ATM machine, which ironically enough was the perfect hiding spot, and wait in seclusion until the delivery boy would enter the lobby of the dorm he was delivering to. He would then run over to the car, which was always left open and running, snatch a box, and dash away down the stairs to the street below. Minutes later he would re-emerge with a marinara-ringed smile, a half-empty box, and a noticeable absence of conscience.

This was not really our style, but I took part in the booty on more than one occasion.

There was a show dedicated to the presentation of new music videos by artists we had convinced ourselves were not mainstream and, therefore, cool. It began at midnight that evening, or the next morning, depending on how you looked at it. We would nearly always time the arrival of the food to coincide with the commencement of the show but would occasionally miscalculate and have to involve ourselves in a game of chance to determine which of us would stay and pay and which would ascend to the room to catch the first clip. I always seemed to lose this gamble and on the rare chance that I didn't, would be faced with the logic that it wasn't my room and hence I could not get in without accompaniment. This never made sense since I would need to be signed in by someone else who lived there anyway.

Tonight, it didn't matter since the order arrived well before we said our goodbyes to the zombies outside and went up to relax and watch intentionally ugly people conduct themselves in choreographed anti-social behavior. From time to time, we would invite others along to share in the custom and, if we felt particularly generous, indulge in a breadstick or half.

Theresa was a girl we had met at a party she was hosting a week or so earlier. Neither of us knew her or really anyone at the party when we arrived, and, in retrospect, I think we appeared there by mistake. She was a very pleasant girl with a young face and very full, darkly painted lips. Her eyes were always wide open which gave her the air of being either really excited or really surprised all of the time. I was sitting on the floor next to the heat monitor when she came over and introduced herself. I had on a grey plaid jacket I had stolen over a baby blue button-up shirt that had once belonged to my father. She commented on the jacket, which gave me an increased feeling of superiority over the global conglomerate I had wronged, and we spoke politely until Brody came over and sat down. He was always steering conversations past the polite and we were enough of a contrast that way to engage most people.

———————————

Very few upperclassmen were ever on the porch for reasons other than passing through and it seemed that Theresa was doing just that when we saw her. She seemed surprised to see us or excited—I couldn't tell on account of the eyes—and eagerly advanced on our position at the bench near the revolving door. I liked her enough to stop and talk if I saw her out, instead of just saying hello or turning while passing to extend the hello to question of current status, but I thought it was a bit presumptuous to invite her up for the show. It was two solid hours and, as we had learned from experience, that can be a little too long to be held captive by someone else's company.

She fervently accepted, and Brody signed us in, me under a pseudonym I borrowed from a movie character and her under her real name; she wasn't that clever and probably assumed that the guard in the glass case had some sort of authority.

The dented metal box of the elevator was filled with the three of us and a wafting mélange of sweet tomato sauce, melted cheese, and the ammoniated cleaners employed to eradicate the streaks of lung butter that covered the walls earlier that morning. It was disgust by association as the ringing vapors lost their sanitary connotation to the unshakable memories of chunky pools and pong. Just as my appetite was departing, the doors cracked open and the elevator spat us forth against Brody's closed door.

The room was small and cluttered with magazines, CD jewel cases, dirty clothes, and sports equipment. The various cleated shoes, pads, sticks, balls, and such belonged to his roommate; I had a difficult time imagining Brody participating in any contact or competitive sports of any kind.

Brody had the ability to possess something for only a few hours and make it appear as if it had been owned and actively used his whole life. Nothing he called his own had the crisp sense of newness or preservation from delicate care. I don't think he ever had to iron and consequently didn't know how, and I stopped him more than once trying to smooth out the wrinkles in a shirt by squatting down and stretching it over his knees.

He was gangly and of moderate good looks. I implied, based on a theory some other friends of mine and I had surmised, that being of moderate good looks was, in fact, more attractive to others since you appeared more accessible and accessibility was inviting by nature. If someone was too handsome, it was off-putting either because one's own waning self-esteem, or because of a general cynicism against those who are perceived to be elite. I tried to exclude myself from any side of this hypothesis once the topic was brought up, but it was an interesting concept.

Theresa was allowed the bed and Brody situated himself on a pile of magazines that may or may not have once had a chair underneath them. He kept sliding off the shiny, beautiful faces and was tearing several pages in the process while I cringed and implored him to just move them. He ignored me and was focusing on Theresa and a conversation about one of her roommates that was making a lethargic attempt at being an actress or something. Theresa seemed to be content talking about the other girl and Brody paused for a second to pull smoke through his cigarette and remind himself that the other girl wasn't here right now, but Theresa was. He exhaled, and I could tell that his fixed regard was back on the present company and that he would as soon as now commence his pushing past the polite to the more curtained regions of conversation.

Theresa seemed keen on exploring such realms and tried vainly, and only fleetingly, to play coy and hesitate while questioning his direction. I had grown increasingly indifferent to her over the last hour and was only now taking any interest in her responses. He was simultaneously hanging on her words and ignoring her while planning his next guided spelunk into her personal affairs. She was not shy.

I added very little to the discussion and my realized fascination in her unabashed candor did little to lighten the increasing weight of it all. I was relieved when the tension broke almost instantly when Brody directed our attention to the tiny glowing box across the room. My eyes were fixed on the screen and I mindlessly echoed their interest in the images while I relocated to the dirty patch of grey comforter next to Theresa. In my inadvertent blindness, I almost missed the edge of the bed entirely and fell to the floor—a bumbling shred of comic relief that would have worked well in furthering the disruption of what should have been awkwardness.

Sometime before the end of the video and prior to the introduction of the next, Brody had lit one of the many candles strewn about amongst the debris. He was always lighting candles and had convinced himself that they were undeniably effective in masking the unpleasantness of his living situation. Most of them were strongly scented and of contrasting aromas, which made for a nauseating blend when their grappling took place in such close, closed quarters.

I was starting to feel sick from the heavy air and from the situation that had developed. The television was off, and I was kissing the thick, coated lips I had watched silently agree to his suggestion. Brody maneuvered in next to her and half covered the two of them with the dirty layers of fabric while his hands disappeared between them.

She tasted like tarnishing metal and I could feel the smear of the dark paste of her lipstick surround my mouth as she bent in contentment. Out of instinct more than raw desire, my hand traveled. A short, but painful flick from the thumb ring he took on and off when he was nervous (or excited) let me know I was venturing on claimed ground. I retreated my handling back across the bare skin above her loosened jeans.

With her prolonged tremor and a clench, it was over.

Brody scurried out into the hallway and Theresa sighed and leaned over to find my turned cheek. I felt like I had swallowed the bitter metal I still tasted and that it lay in a heap, lugging my insides towards my feet. I was sick now.

It was silent except for the sound of running water down the hall and I sat up and faced the wall. Brody reappeared what seemed like hours later and turned on the harsh reality of the fluorescent light over the desk. He picked a piece of the coagulated cheese off the cardboard box on the floor and turned the television back on.

Theresa announced that she guessed she should be heading home and thanked us both for a memorable evening. Paying her just enough attention to respond, Brody suggested that I walk her home. If he were aware in any way of my reaction or current disposition, he would have known what a horrible act of betrayal he had committed by sentencing me to the long, uncomfortable walk back to her apartment, which was in the exact opposite direction of my home. He had dismissed everyone and everything in the room except for himself and the television and was even then beginning to lose interest in the television.

We took the stairs down to the lobby and she made sure to remind me to sign out, still believing that harm would somehow come to those whose visits were documented as eternal.

Her street was poorly lit and smelled of garbage and urine. All the roadside shrubs were dead or dying and all the houses, including hers, were adorned with single pieces of kitchen or living room furniture that had been exiled to their respective front porches. The pang of copper still clung in my mouth and I was sicker than ever, though I knew that my mind was sending the illness to my stomach now.

We reached the broken sidewalk and bent iron railing of her steps and I turned to go. She grabbed a half fist of grey plaid and pulled me around against her. I opened my mouth, hoping in vain to expel the taste back into hers, but it only intensified and ran like liquid down to my belly. She laughed and ran her sleeve across my lips when she noticed that I hadn't bothered to wipe away the dark smears from before. She simpered a goodnight and I slipped off the curb to cross to the other side, trying not to look back.

VIII

It was night and I went running. Running at night is a wonderful activity for a few reasons, the first being the noticeable absence of that big ball of glowing radiation in the sky. It was still pretty warm tonight but not to the point where you wanted to rid yourself of clothing layers a few blocks into your route. The other plus was the feeling of superiority you got from passing all the stiffs who were just going out to drink or coming home from studying. It was probably the same sensation that Army guys or the crew team would get when they saw you in the hallway rubbing your eyes and they had already accomplished more while you were sleeping than you would all day. Some of the people I passed might have even been running earlier that morning and maybe farther than I was planning on going, but I was screaming past them now and that's all that mattered to me.

I liked to set out with no destination in mind and then head for where I determined was the greatest probability of me seeing people I knew. It was very satisfying to yell a salutation at someone and then follow it with a refusal to stop and chat to avoid breaking stride. I also ran much faster if I knew someone was watching.

The slush of my nylon pants whispered along with the spray nozzle of a shopkeeper who was bullying a sheen of soapy water into the street. He caught me on the leg with the stream and the synthetic fabric hugged my leg for the next few blocks until it dried in the now cooling night air. I decided at that moment to go see Idelle.

It was because of an incident one night when she came over to sleep in my bed that she popped into my head just then. I had gotten off of work that evening and met her on my way home just down from my dorm in front of the emergency room entrance of the hospital that consumed the block across the street. It wasn't an unusually eventful night and I hadn't eaten an abnormally excessive amount of the frozen cookie dough from the freezer, but I was wound up. I don't know how she didn't slap me on the way up from the lobby because, in retrospect, I was being annoying, playing grab-ass in the elevator and all. I would pinch her just below the back pocket of her plaid pants and then run to one side and thrust myself into the metal wall and then run over and do the same to the other side until the heavy box was swinging and scraping the shaft. She was laughing and telling me to stop, but I could tell that she didn't mean it. She never wanted me to stop doing anything stupid and her laugh was intoxicating, so I wouldn't quit on my own. We were like a performer and audience with just the two of us and it never mattered if anyone else ever enjoyed the show.

When we stopped on one of the floors (I had pressed all the buttons and she still laughed), a tall girl in pajama bottoms and a sweatshirt got on and looked around the pendulum of a car with a confused, mortified look. She didn't appear comfortable asking what the problem was and got off on the next floor. I grabbed Idelle and tried to kiss her, but she was laughing and squirming about.

About five minutes into the show we were watching from my bed, the internal vibrations were becoming increasingly less fun for me and Idelle began to get concerned for my health. I had no explanation for my state, but I stopped her in mid-question and stated that I would be right back. I put on my white running shoes with the blue stripe and a pair of gossamer soccer shorts that were truly pornographic when it was windy or raining, and I took off.

That was that night and although I made it up to her when I returned several miles later and although we hadn't been that same successful comedy exhibition for some time now, I really wanted to see her tonight.

She lived a ways down off campus in a dirty part of town that seemed to be populated solely by second and third-year college students and their drug dealers. It was not uncommon to see someone taking out the trash from a third-floor apartment by releasing it off their fire escape where it had little to no chance of staying inside the bag upon its descent. The smell of the streets and curbs seeped into your being, but my stride wouldn't let it settle long enough to penetrate.

Her building was on one of the only well-lit streets and her room was on the side next to the lamp post. It took me a moment of clarity to realize that this little drop-in was occurring on a school night and it was late already when I set out. I didn't know of any tangible objections her roommates had with me, but I didn't want to call up from the lobby and wake them up and give them cause for persuading her against me.

Not thinking at first about the romance of it, I picked up a particle of the pavement that had shaken loose from a pothole and chucked it at her window. I didn't want to break it so I tossed it lightly and, overestimating my strength, I missed completely. I found a slightly larger stone and managed to hit the scrawl of spray paint just below her room. Finally, I connected, and I was very surprised to see her emerge only seconds after the first tink of rock against glass. So surprised, in fact, that I nearly hit her with the rock that was already on its way to serve as my follow-up knock. She, of course, laughed.

She was squinting from the yellow light of the lamp post and the roundness of her cheeks was tight against her crinkled brow. She denied it but was obviously sleeping when she came to see what lunatic was summoning her to the window.

Nicholas J. Stevens

When I met her at her door after bounding up every other stair of the three flights up, I surmised that she must have been up to have answered so quickly. She admitted that she was sleeping (but wanted me to stay) and got up and for some unknown, supernatural reason, went to the window to see me.

I don't fully understand the process of dreaming or the transition from subconscious to the other kind, but I know I have awoken suddenly from a dream that incorporated a sound or feeling from something in the real world a split moment before I felt or heard it. A mind could go mad on it, but I knew what she meant it and believed it.

She had readjusted to the darkness of her apartment and recoiled in the glare of the hallway lights outside her door. The skin under her eyes was a pallid blue and it blended nicely with the perpetual glow of her face. She blinked quickly a few times and put her head on my beating chest as if to mimic her return to sleep. With her still resting, she patted me on the shoulder and led me inside by my hand.

When I stopped her and kissed her next to the bar in the kitchen, it was the only time I saw the enormity of her blue eyes that night. She held the look of shock for only a second and then laughed before returning the gesture.

IX

I remember naps as a kid as squeezing my eyes as tightly together as I could until they stayed together on their own, and I was exhausted enough by the process to fall asleep. As I grew up and out of just listening to and obeying my parents for the sole reason of doing so, I would smuggle comic books under my pillow or between the side of the dark wooden bunk bed and the wall. I anticipated napping just for the opportunity to be defiant in my reading. It was probably the most rebellious thing I did so it could easily be said that I was a pretty good kid.

It's difficult to remember lying down in the middle of the day—while the sun transformed the curtains into a lamp shade and the room glowed with the amber of muffled light—as a bad thing. There were hours when I longed for the subtle peace of lying on top of a made bed and drifting off while fully dressed. That, to me, was a nap.

I tried to remind myself on the rare nights when I was bitten by insomnia of the stolen minutes beneath my office desk, stretched sideways under the hollow metal drawers and trying desperately to find the perfect angle to ease the stress of my hip against the hard, unpadded floor. I would have given anything during those moments spent staring up at the UPC stickers I tacked under my workstation to have the pillow I cursed for its imagined rigidity when sleep would not visit me. I would have traded my lunch hour and both episodes of *The Wonder Years* I watched during it for the embrace of the bed I tossed in when no position was comfortable and when the realization hit that

Nicholas J. Stevens

squeezing my eyes shut no longer worked. I was lucky. It wasn't often that I couldn't sleep at night, but it was probably because I didn't nap nearly as much as I wished.

When the offer was extended to partake in the joy of afternoon slumber, I was eager to flatten the mattress. Mandy suggested it and since I had to pretend it was a joke after my offer for all of us (Mandy, Julia, and I) share one of the double beds was declined, I climbed in with her and Julia adjourned to the bed across the room.

She was a sprightly girl with short, curly blonde hair and small round lips. She had enough of an overbite to be endearing without ever looking goofy—which can happen in some instances—and was much more prone to subtle trifles than Julia. Any outright flirting would have been embarrassingly exposed by Julia and so we were forced to steal looks and only assume what the other thought. As a result, we were always unsure of where we stood, even after I leapt into bed next to her.

I almost sank right through the thick comforter and sifted out onto the ground beneath the bed. It was like being hugged by a very beautiful fat woman, the pillow being the flat roundness of her bosom.

Mandy was lying on her back and I on my side with my arm draped across her stomach and the bottom few of her ribs. I could hear the discomfort of her short, forced breaths and slid my forearm down across the curve of her hip. She sighed in agreement.

She had on a flowery house dress from a thrift store I introduced her to when the three of us and my roommate went home for a weekend a few weeks earlier. It was a small pattern and looked busy from far away, but I was close enough now to appreciate the detail of the petals and leaves.

I was a few inches away from her cheek, just out of reach of the extended curl, trying to avoid being tickled by the unkempt hair. One strand had found its way onto my nose and I detected a whisper of a scowl when I pulled away from her hip momentarily to brush it off. I promptly returned my half embrace and moved into the mess of curls so that no one strand could irritate me. I was next to her ear and my nose was flat against the small tab that partially covered the opening above her small, studded lobe.

She shifted slightly towards me and the graze of my eyelashes made her head wince and cheek swell in a faint smile. Her eyes were still closed, and I had yet to see the inside of my own when I moved closer still with the apprehension of a tourist looking for an unknown street in an unfamiliar town. I knew that it was the pleasantness of anticipation and not the disgust of frustration that directed her lack of direct reciprocation.

I moved closer and felt the tip of my nose slide around into the crease where the flap of hers met her now flushed cheek.

She readjusted, and I could feel her hot breath shift from her nose to her mouth as she closed her lips and swallowed. As her mouth reopened the pleat of her upper lip grazed mine and she closed them again. I pushed her head gently with mine and enclosed the bulb of her bottom lip between mine. With this, she pulled in the sides of her mouth and extended the softness of our first undeniable kiss. I cupped my hand around her hip, pulled her to me, and accepted the certainty of it.

X

Emily had given notice and since I had a rule about not seeing co-workers or, more appropriately, not seeing co-workers less than clothed, I gave myself permission to notice Emily. After she stated she was leaving, the last two weeks saw our previously harmless flirting intensify to attempt to force some sort of event or culmination. It might have been obvious to her, though it wasn't really to me, that I would not pursue her beyond the boundaries of frequent, planned interaction (in this case, work).

She was not my idea of physically pretty, but she had a magnetic fun about her the same way board games can be fun to reluctant teenagers once they abandon their image of elitist cool. She laughed a lot and I took great pleasure out of making others laugh, especially those I respected or liked in some form.

I would point out any flaw in spoken word or action she would make and make light of it in an emblematic pigtail-pulling of the girl I wouldn't admit I liked. She would laugh loudly and swing for my arm or back as I cringed and ducked away. This contact became more frequent and we became very comfortable in each other's personal space.

I was asked to accept the responsibility of management and move to the other store across town about a year prior. I had no formal education in the field or any supervisory experience of any kind, so when I agreed, I did so determined to lead by character because it was really all I knew. This led to the self-imposed rule against working relationships. It seemed to me to be both publicly noble and to administer simple common sense as the best way to preclude any dramatic situations that might ensue. But I was still a young man and one who was Machiavellian in my ability to rationalize and bargain with my own mind. The way I perceived it, as soon as she formally asserted her intent to depart, she was no longer under obligation of employment, no longer subject to the rules of the organization, no longer under my jurisdiction as supervisor, and, therefore, an ordinary citizen who could be treated as such. This applied to romantic ventures because the possibilities suited me, but didn't apply to stealing, not cleaning the bathrooms, et cetera.

The last night we worked together was the last night she worked at all and there was still no lock on plans outside the confines and safety of the shop. There was no acknowledgement of any tension and the evening had seemed disappointingly un-eventful until I evacuated the contents of the chocolate pump into the filling dish sink below. She snatched my unsuspecting hand and playfully, but forcefully, stuck it into the stream of dark brown syrup. It covered my hand and the thumb side of my forearm up to nearly my elbow.

I curled my lips in exaggerated anger and whipped a cursive line of mocha past her head onto the wall behind. She laughed and thrust her hands into the stainless-steel vessel where the stalwart remains of the fleeting sugary stew still clung to its walls. They reemerged coated and headed straight for my face, which was now wearing a pronounced look of shock and terror.

I managed to take hold of her wrists and compel them to the running water next to us. I held them there long enough to disarm the offending mocha while Emily writhed in my grasp, screaming and laughing. I let her go and she cupped enough water to douse my apron and collar while pretending to be angry herself. We paused, staring at each other, half-smiling, readjusting this way or that to avoid the clench of our dampened clothing, and waiting for the other to act or speak.

———

I sat on the floor of my room facing the wall-sized closet and the vast mirror that ran its length. Emily sat on top of me, astride, kissing my mouth and neck. My head had fallen to my shoulder as her open mouth moved to the opposite one. My eyes wearily opened and focused on the mirror several feet away. I stared at the wide, pale hump that occluded me and the unfinished curls on the back of the head that was anxiously moving over me. My stillness caught her attention and she stopped.

She leaned back in my view and asked me what was wrong. I gave no reply and lowered my head to avoid her fallen brow, as if trying to literally duck the question. She repeated it as I shifted, starting to get up. I was shaking my head and shrugging both the shoulder that was cradling my head and the one that was becoming cold from her evaporating saliva.

"I don't know. I'm just weird sometimes. I don't know."

The lackluster explanation ushered out her confusion and led in her deserved anger.

I was looking at the reflection of the adjacent wall in the mirror as she got dressed and moved to leave, hesitating only to shrug herself and point a look of disdain in my direction.

XI

All day I had been responding to inquiries about my Valentine's Day plans with a claim that my date was short, stout, and full of gin. It would also be made of glass and eventually combined with tonic, but I withheld that detail in the interest of comic timing.

I was, as they say, talking out of my ass since I managed to make it through high school and the entirety of my college career, which only turned out to be two years, without consuming so much as a drop of alcohol. A few points to clarify: 1) I didn't drink in grade school, either and 2) I did used to go to church when I still thought it made a difference as to what kind of a person you were and were to become and we drank little silver cups of wine during that part when they tell you it's Jesus' blood (that made sense). Other than that, I was straight-edge. I didn't know I was until I got to college and someone branded me with the title. I didn't put any black marker X's on my forearms or go to meetings and I didn't haze any drunk kids...much. In fact, all my friends either drank or smoked things or dropped things or ate things or whatever. They were just generally more fun to be around, when they didn't get creeped out by having someone around who was sober.

I initially had no intention of drinking, but thought it was a good thing to say since, in lieu of a date or even a prospect of one, all I had was a sneer and an appearance I tried way too hard to keep up. I sought to play the misanthrope and act like I was doing it out of cynicism, but I would have liked to have gotten dressed up in a suit (I had collected many from various thrift stores with veritably no occasions to wear them) and slung a beautiful girl

Nicholas J. Stevens

from my arm like a jacket on a hot night. At the time being, however, I had only a leisurely physical liaison in its early stages and that isn't the type of thing that should be incubated by such a grandiose occasion. It means a lot to some people, me probably included, to be someone else's Valentine's date.

After repeating the intention over and over all day, I went home to Will. Actually, I met Will on the way home. He pulled the string on my back by asking and I, with the predictability of a child's doll, retorted, "et cetera, et cetera, a bottle of gin." Unlike those from the shop who were friendly enough to ask but not friends enough to know, Will knew I didn't drink. He was also one of the few partaking friends that never pressured me to be the first to share the wine.

He politely let me finish my ramblings, paused a moment, and asked, "Why not?"

At exactly that point, the good reasons I had spent my life reinforcing could not be summoned to my mind or mouth. Even the lousy, weak reasons like, "My mom might call, and I would sound drunk," were nowhere to be found. I doubt she would care. So, the critical part of my brain, the part that kept me objective by playing the devil's, jerk's, tough guy's, conservative's, or whoever's advocate jumped all over it.

Yeah, why not?

Will insisted on buying the portly green bottle in honor of this momentous occasion. I had money, which made having no date all the worse, but it was no good to Will. Dusk was holding off the ever-stretching daylight that was tired of being restricted the past season-and-a-half and I stood outside the liquor store waiting for Will. I was not of age and although I was reasonably sure you did not have to be any specific age to go into a liquor store, I opted to stay outside and be surprised by what I had sent him in to get.

I proclaimed at the onset of the evening that I probably had a pretty high tolerance since I had observed during family gatherings that most of my blood were accustomed to being so with an impressive level of alcohol in them. Will was now playing the role of my critical brain, as he did instinctively and without effort, and questioned whether it was genetics or rehearsal that gave them their ability to function. As was usually the case, I would have lost the argument, so I pretended to be absorbed in the logistics of preparing my first cocktail and ignored his rightness.

We had a small, white paper bag with two-litre bottles of tonic and just enough clean glasses for the two of us. Alas, we had forgotten the limes. Oh, the limes!

Fortunately, if we needed food or silverware, we lived above the restaurant where I worked. Unfortunately, if we wanted to sleep or to live without six-legged roommates who not only did not pay rent but ate and performed all steps of the mating process wherever they pleased, we lived above the restaurant where I worked. It was a piece of good fortune in this case.

Margo was working, and I slinked in with a smirk that could have meant any number of things on Valentine's Day. She noticed and pulled up the bottom lids of her eyes to attempt to decipher, by my look alone, what I was up to.

"Can I borrow a few limes?"

"Limes? For what?" She smiled.

"Just to have. I don't want to get scurvy."

"Nicholas...Are you drinking?"

"No! Well, not without the limes."

She shook her head and smiled wider so that the boldness of her white teeth shone between her painted lips. She inquired as to my plans once I acquired the limes, and I went into much greater detail to her about having no date (except Will) and how it was finally time to get into a bottle.

To be kind as a friend and flirty as a bartender, which is hard to turn off when on the clock, she said that she would be my Valentine. She even gave me a sticker with a train and hearts on it that someone had given to her earlier that day. It made me feel like I was on a fast elevator. It would have been out of place and excruciatingly awkward to pick that moment to declare my love, so I just thanked her for the sticker and the citrus and went back upstairs.

Will had moved the operation up to his room in front of the television. My room was a canvas of once-worn clothing (still clean) laid over my mattress and an armoire that, when stood up as intended, was at a perpetual 30-degree angle. This forced any entertaining into Will's much cleaner and much larger room. Also, he had the Sega hockey.

As a painful reminder of my inferior abilities on the pixilated ice, we recorded our ongoing statistics on the hallway wall between our rooms. It was in big black marker that would mock me every time I walked to a game or away from what was usually a defeat. The crudely drawn cat that signified tied games was locked in an expression of curiosity that seemed to ask, "Why? Why are you still intent on playing? Look at the tally thus far!" How the face of that cat taunted me!

All the songs I repeated in the shower and on my lengthy walks about town told me that I would like gin, but I was nervous more about the possibility of disliking it than I was about intentionally losing control of my mind for the first time. My anxiety was quelled as the first sip washed through my mouth like clean linen being spread over my tongue and tucked underneath. With the issue of taste filed away, my concern turned to the secondary worry about getting too drunk and doing something derogatory to my mental, social, or physical health. That, too, was fleeting as I reminded myself that I was in the custody of a stand-up guy and the best friend I ever had. He had resigned to drink only enough to dispel the discomfort I am sure my other friends felt when they were leaving sobriety behind, and I was inviting it along where it was not welcome.

After several drinks and a similar toll of hockey matches, we went for cheesesteaks. There was no decision made to do so, rather it was an inevitability, like going to the bathroom or brushing your teeth before going to bed. The venue of choice was nothing more than a seedy dump about two miles or so from our seedy dump. Despite being mid-February, it was not terribly cold and so our responsible decision to walk was an easy one to make.

We set out and I began speaking. The average speed of a healthy man on foot is approximately three miles an hour, making our trip and my continuous babbling about 45 minutes, had it stopped when we reached the establishment. It did not. It was not incoherent, which would have probably been easier to tolerate— just incessant, unremitting, unbroken talk. Talk to Will. Talk at Will. Talk to the lovely Joann (who just wanted our order). Talk at the lovely Joann. Apologies to the lovely Joann. Talk to people at the next table I met once or didn't. Talk to myself when everyone else's ears were so full of words, they were spilling back out and running down their necks.

The soft bread filled with greasy meat and cheese and the thick, soggy fries pushed the approaching unpleasant point of intoxication back a few steps, keeping it at just jolly and fun, instead of nauseous and stumbling. It was important that it be a pleasant experience so that I would anticipate repeating it.

We paid the lovely Joann and I piled up a mound of bills on the table under my empty plate. I knew that this, and not my relentless verbal apologies, was the only true way to express my gratitude for her patience. Seeing the remaining grease slide down the tilting plate away from her stack of cash, she smiled a genuine smile that I wasn't sure came from my exit, appreciation of my monetary gesture, or her being smitten by tipsy charm. The gin told me it was the latter, but I was increasingly skeptical on the walk home.

We stopped by the dorms on our way home (at my request) to see if my budding physical liaison was interested in blossoming further tonight. I should have been surprised that she was home and should have realized that the leisure of our relationship may not have been as relaxed as I saw it.

She was a self-proclaimed straight-edge girl herself and only after she kissed me hello did it occur to me that she might be put off by my wafting of gin. She didn't mention it and seemed happy to be walking hand in hand to spend Valentine's Eve on some once-worn clothes next to an armoire that didn't stand up straight.

XII

Jane had a baby that wasn't mine. It couldn't have been mine, and not in the talk show way where someone says that it couldn't be theirs because they are fighting it until the lab results are revealed by the self-satisfied host and their jaw drops open and the flabbergasted father whose life has just changed for the much worse looks off camera in defeat, sometimes shaking his spinning head while thinking only how it will affect him and never of his child. No, not in that kind of way.

I had never been with Jane. I had never even held her hand. It is discouraging to hear what people will assume based on mere public interaction. I used to wait for her after gym class and walk her to what I think was the less-advanced version of chemistry, but there were no sweaty fits of rubbing and pressing in janitor's closets or underneath stairs. I wasn't even sure that type of thing really went on, for I never saw it.

Barbara called her weird, as did everyone who didn't know her and that was pretty much everybody. Barbara was weird, too, but in a fun kind of way and she didn't have a right to care or make her opinion known anyway. She was leaving just enough of herself in my life to make it hard and she was doing a good job of that.

Jane was plain by sight, with straight, light brown hair that had just enough red in it to only be noticeable when she moved suddenly, which she never really did. If an archaeologist discovered a picture of her, he would never know when it was taken. She wore clothes that weren't representative of any particular time period, only not at all representative of the present. They were stripes and faded t-shirts that looked like they went straight to thrift stores without ever stopping off anywhere new.

You had to lean in to hear anything she said because it never went above a whisper and she lowered her head when she spoke. It was even more difficult because you had to fall past her eyes, which pulled in your gaze like swirling water around and eventually down a drain, to get to her mouth. I suppose that is why, to the outside observer, it would look like two entranced lovers whose heads are drawn together by the magnetism of their love. In truth, I did like her, but I just couldn't hear her.

She wrote to me a few times when I went away to school and I showed her letters and drawings to friends in jest. They were written with the shaky hand of a determined, but frail child and the drawings were usually in crayon and depicted her in a rainbow pond with a beaming version of me that looked like a smiling lollypop. I realized that my attempts to make others understand the virtue in them fell short and they were just laughing at her. I kept them in my desk from then on and quickly dismissed the subject when someone stumbled across them and asked questions that couldn't quickly be answered.

The romantic exploits of my initial year of college and freedom were awkward and memorable for the wrong reasons. I vowed to take a hiatus from idyll and went to work at a summer camp that eventually became the only job I ever walked out on. Avoiding intimacy there was easy since all the girl counselors were either snatched up the first day by those with initiative or they were ugly in both character and appearance. The only other females present were the campers and they were at least a year or two younger than what could be reasonably deemed appealing with a clear conscience.

She never mentioned being with child or being with anyone in a situation that would produce a child and I had no idea until I returned home the next summer. Friend pickings were slim, and the scarcity made me take on company that was on the fringes of people I only scarcely knew to begin with. The gangly brother of a kid I played soccer with asked if I had "fucked her" and wondered whether the baby was mine. I interrupted the ugliness of his follow-up story about her gagging on some other friend of his by stating again that I only knew her as a friend. I lanced him with my "no," but he barely felt it and rattled on. I was blurred by the blend of images in my head of her losing her goodness to some sweaty, weak-limbed teenage shopping mall rebel and the violence of hitting the messenger until my hands turned his sunken face into a weeping, bloody mess. I said nothing and turned my back on them to leave. The scrawny one yelled something that I made myself hear as something else that further fueled my hatred for him.

I called her a few days later and asked to see her and maybe spend some time together at the park nearby. She was living with her grandparents and they were understandably very hesitant to allow visitors, especially of the male persuasion. She only alluded to the whereabouts of her mother and never mentioned her father at all. Her grandparents seemed to be caring people with her best interest in mind but were too slow to serve as a formidable opponent to their granddaughter or her friends.

She was very pleased to see me and growing increasingly impatient as her grandpa and I spoke at length about the city where I went to school and its history. I could tell that she wanted to leave there both immediately and for good, but I was the only one of us that understood the importance of allowing her guardians time to gain at least a little trust in me, if not her.

She had a large box that had once held fishing tackle that now served as her art case and transporter of personal creations. From it she produced a road safety-themed coloring book and two boxes of crayons—one consisting of standard colors and the other comprised of metallic jewel tones. We took a spot on one of the picnic tables and searched for a suitable pair of pages that we could work on together.

I was drawing flames on a non-descript, rounded automobile whose driver I had already bequeathed with a hearty pair of black sideburns. She was outlining the lips of a woman standing at a bus stop with the ruby crayon and beginning to draw the cross-hatching of a pair of fishnet stockings.

"She's a whore," she said and laughed lowly.

"At least she's looking both ways before she walks the street."

She laughed again, and I suggested that we leave shortly before the sun went down and we were kicked out of the park.

Light abandoned us in a hurry, so much so that I hadn't noticed the consuming black and was driving around without my lights on until the second time a car flashed its high beams. Not at all wanting to take her home or to go home myself, we took turns giving directions to turn down foreign streets to get lost.

College had gotten me used to deciding when it was bedtime, if at all, and I had difficulty adjusting. My parents were pleasantly accepting by imposing no curfew, but it was a futile gesture since everyone I knew still had one. Jane certainly did and although I could tell by her grandfather's lack of certainty when he said it that it had been extended on account of our conversation, the thought of it was driving the budgeting of our time in my head.

We finally found a spot in a shallow field that seemed like the place where cars would stack up if there were a major event nearby. There was no shifty fat guy in a fluorescent vest motioning to us, but we found a resting place for my parents' large sedan.

The insects were deafening, and I already had a hard time hearing her even with the car off. She spoke even lower than normal and mistook my steep lean as a movement for affection, not a crutch for my sense of hearing. She tilted her chin up and we kissed. She slid back into the embracing leather seat and I followed into her mouth.

I wanted to ask her if she was okay and if we were okay, but I desperately wanted to avoid any of the reasons why we wouldn't be. She kissed and grabbed my back and shoulders while occasionally stopping to laugh again the way she laughed at the ridiculous drawing of the whore in the safety book. I was confused, but confusion did little to obstruct the other feelings.

We were outside behind the car when she laid back on the trunk and held my hands to her sides. We had been fully clothed until this point and hidden from all light except the momentary interest of a lone passing car. Now in the open, we were exposed by the yellow lamp hanging overhead.

My hands moved across the openings of her pockets towards each other until cornering upwards before meeting. The stripes came together, and a clearing of skin grew in front of me. She did nothing to encourage except to not discourage it at all.

With her shirt up past the slanting fabric of her bra, I could see the exhausted flesh where life once grew. I stopped.

Still holding her hands, I pulled her up and into my arms. I told her we had better go and if we ever wanted to be together again, she needed to get back even the slightest bit early. As she did on the trunk, she agreed by saying nothing.

Back at home, I parked the car and looked back to watch the garage door being lowered like a hood over our large family automobile. My eyes shot wide open and I ducked back under the falling metal door in time to avoid its collapse. I could see clearly in the stark light of the garage an outline of a back and arms drawn in moisture on the trunk. I wiped it dry with the sleeve of my shirt and turned back towards the house and a night of old sitcoms.

XIII

I gave Natty a pair of green corduroy pants that I bought for a quarter and brought back from home. I had never worn them, and they asked me every time I opened my bottom pants drawer why they were there. I had a hard time coming up with new answers.

They fit her well, but not in the traditional sense, and stayed in place somehow by hanging slightly off her hips. This made me realize they would have looked nothing short of ridiculous on me... even more ridiculous than a pair of bright green corduroy pants normally would...if such a thing were ever normal.

They weren't the hunter green of hotel lobby couches or of collared sweaters from outdoor stores in the mall. They were a shade or so bluer than the green grass on the other side of the fence might be. They were ghastly, but she said that she liked green and she had been wearing green and never anything new, just new to her, every time I had seen her.

She was in a writing class of mine and was the only person I really spoke to when class was over. I often addressed the others in the class when we read "anonymous" contributions and offered our analyses and amateurish critiques. It spoiled the mystery when you stared directly and intently at the writer and told them your thoughts, but it was like proving you were smarter than those who didn't pick up on it. After the first week or so, all of the observant students knew each other's writing styles and since it was drilled into us to "find a voice and stick with it," no one dared to wander, and cause confusion and the cycle of targeted reviews went on.

I only signed up for it to force myself into doing something creative in a positive atmosphere. I was never interested in reading or hearing anyone else's work, including Natty's. I liked her as a person and as a distraction from the mundane sci-fi stories and obvious mysteries that ate up a few scheduled hours of my week. She was lean and looked taller than she was, and her face was an agreeable contrast of pale skin and freckles, interrupted by strands of abnormally dyed, blood red hair. It could be said that she was "my style" by someone who thought that I had one, but I had a difficult time being madly attracted to her despite my self-imposed persuasion.

I invited her to do things and hung out with her in her room, but it was time spent of unfamiliarity, like when a neighbor from down the hall ambles into your open door and sits on top of a chair, instead of in it, while talking to you.

She came over late in the afternoon. I suppose it was evening since it was darkening, but it was winter and so that was just late afternoon. She liked to draw, and I didn't really want to see any of her drawings either, but she brought a book-full and it gave us an excuse to lay on the floor and look through them while searching for an empty page to violate.

It was snowing pretty hard and ever since Idelle took her television back, I had lost all contact with the uninteresting, but necessary information like weather and elections. It was supposed to keep snowing for a long time and at a pace that renders travel by any means but foot unthinkable, and even that would be a trial.

Without mention, she laid her shin across the back of my ankle and rested it there while her shoes dried next to the vent across the room. Her socks were striped with non-repeating colors and still modestly wet themselves.

I was impressed by the fact that she wasn't wearing the corduroys as I had determined that such a move would be a little corny and worthy of an eye-rolling and the inaudible sound it makes when your mouth falls open in disgust and you want to keep it private.

My window faced the other three sides of the quad and they were invisible now behind the mantle of white that was lowered from the grey clouds above. No one was going anywhere and we both knew it. This acceptance we handled with the most familiarity and comfort of any situation we had encountered.

I offered my toothbrush and a pair of flannel pajama pants that were very big, along with a t-shirt that had once represented something called "Bowhunter Day" at an archery range somewhere in 1985. This combination made her look even taller since the pants sat even lower than the others, and only then with the critical help of a drawstring did they stay on at all. The shirt was consequently just long enough to cover the top of the pinched rolls of the flannel waste so long as neither side was raised by a bend of the other. It looked good and although I had no premonition or desire for it to occur at the onset of the evening (or afternoon), we were going to be sharing sheets.

I wasn't going to sleep on the floor and I wasn't going to make her sleep on the floor and I will wholeheartedly admit that a lean, warm body was always superior to the stuffed reminder of my high school sweetheart, but I didn't eagerly want what I figured she did. I offered, nonetheless.

I tried to do it with the same nonchalance of our initial acceptance of Mother Nature's match making, but the effort to seem casual was still effort and it shone through as an invitation for more than just an innocuous winter slumber...as I'm sure the arm laying across her side did and as I'm sure my shifting back against the wall to avoid pressing against her a very clear invitation did. But the bed was small, and it is infinitely more relaxed to lay an arm over and not to tuck it under yourself and, as we learned by the weather, nature does what it wants and some things you simply can't control.

In what was surely the last bit of evidence of my clear, yet absent intentions, I had put on the music to which I routinely fell asleep. Given its purpose, it was a musical glacier—slow, epic, tranquil. My feeling was that it was beneficial to the level of familiarity by revealing to her a process that is one of a person's most private, preparing for sleep, but also, I meant not to change any of my habits because she was there.

I was leaden with sleep and sliding towards its inviting and subtle embrace when she rolled over to face me. My eyes refused their commands to open like a pouting child who disobeyed its parents. I felt her lips against mine and our mouths join. My hand settled in between the blades of her shoulders and ushered her flush against me. Another half turn and I was veiled in the blood red hair. The flannel accordion had extended itself flat again and was resting at a slant down past her hip. I pulled a fist of it back up, but my weariness made it like lead as well and it fell back to my side, pulling its contents with it against me.

Sleep was on me like a leather blanket and the music was slowing to a slur like stirring cooling syrup. I moved, if at all, only out of instinct as consciousness submitted to its overpowering and more shapeless counterpart.

XIV

Me: "Hey, turn that down, will you?"

B: "That's Prince!"

Me: "Yeah, I know. Believe me, I can hear."

A: "I met her in a hotel lobby masturbating with a magazine..."

Me: "You're insane. Can we...ah, never mind."

B: "What was up with you tonight?"

Me: "What do you mean?"

B: "You're a magnet! It was incredible."

Me: "Shut up. You're an idiot."

A: "That's when Nikki started to cry!"

Me: "Thank you for the volume control. I don't know what you're talking about."

A: "Who was that girl that grabbed you when we came in?"

Me: "Her name's Chirpy. It was her place."

A: "What?!?"

B: "What's her name?"

Me: "Her name's Chirpy, like a bird noise or whatever."

B: "Why do they call her Chirpy?"

A: "Is that her real name?"

Me: "As far as I know that's her real name, but I've never seen her license or birth certificate or anything. I never even really met her until tonight."

A: "She seemed to know you."

Me: "I think she thinks she does. She told some people I was bisexual. I don't even know her."

A: "You never told us. How did she find out?"

Me: "Asshole. I never even met her and her and her fat friend, Olivia, told some people I liked dudes, too, and Clayton heard it and told me."

A: "Were you two in bed when he told you? Like afterwards, you know?"

B: "Stop it! Get off the horn! We're going to get pulled over!"

A: "Yeah right, people get pulled over for honking their horn." Right there! Whew! Yeah!"

B: "I'm not driving anymore with you. You're walking."

Me: "Anyway, dicks, I don't even know Chirpy or her fat friend, Olivia, and they are spreading malicious lies about me and then stupid Chirpy kisses me on the cheek when she sees me at her stupid party. What a fucking phony."

B: "Yeah, you don't like girls."

Me: "Honestly, I hate you both."

A: "But you were talking to another girl."

B: "Several girls! He was a magnet!"

Me: "Please stop that. Which one?"

B: "See! He can't even keep them straight!"

A: "He can't even keep himself straight. Aaaaahhhh."

B: "Oh shit."

Me: "I'm going to fly over this seat and steer us into an oncoming bus. I swear to God."

B: "You could have kicked us down a little something at least, one of the exiles from your harem."

Me: "I'm ignoring you now...Are you talking about Oriel?"

A: "How the hell would I know? The dark-haired one you were talking to by the door."

"Yeah, Oriel. What about her?"

A: "What was up?"

Me: "Yeah, that didn't work out. She left with somebody else."

A: "What about the blonde girl?"

Me: "Which one?"

B: "A magnet!"

Me: "I'm seriously looking for a bus right now. Where's the 67A? It should be along any minute."

A: "The blonde one with the blue thing on."

Me: "She had weird eyes, like nocturnal animal eyes."

B: "So what? What was up?"

Me: "Well, that's who she left with."

A: "That's who who left with?"

B: "Jackass, listen to the story. She left with the other girl he was talking to. And stop touching the wheel when I'm driving!"

A: "She left with the other girl? Like 'left with' the other girl?"

Me: "Yes. I was talking to Oriel and then she went off somewhere and the other girl came up and said she worked down the street from the coffee shop and walks by every day and said that she had a crush on me."

B: "A magnet! That's my boy!"

Me: "I was trying to talk to her, but she was all hammered and those weirdo ferret eyes were all glassed over and staring all weird at me. She said something about knowing Oriel and seeing me talking to her and then I asked where she was and if she had seen her."

B: "Stop! Do not touch the horn again! I'm fucking serious! I'm taking the fuse out when we get back."

Me: "She said she 'just got on her' in the bathroom."

A: "What?!? What does that mean?"

B: "What do you think?"

Me: "She just got on her. I don't know. I guess it means what it sounds like."

A: "What did you do?"

Me: "What was I going to do? I said, 'oh, great.'"

A: "What did she say?"

Me: "She didn't say anything. She was hammered. She was trying to find a mouse to eat or something."

A: "What?"

B: "The eyes. Listen."

Me: "Then Oriel showed up."

B: "Oh shit. What happened?"

Me: "Nothing, really. We were next to the door and the ferret girl went out into the stairwell."

A: "Where were we?"

Me: "Do I know? You were probably next in line to make out in the bathroom together. Ask Chirpy, she'll tell you. I think you were still on the couch."

A: "I thought you said they left together."

Me: "Yeah, so Oriel is all close and says that she's leaving and kisses me. Like a kiss, too. It was long."

B: "Do we need to stop for anything? I don't want to get there and then go back out."

A: "That's awesome. Where was the other girl?"

Me: "Like I said, she went into the stairwell and when we stopped kissing, I followed her out."

A: "Why didn't you go with them?"

Me: "I asked, but Oriel said next time."

B: "What? What is that?"

Me: "I don't know. I asked."

A: "That's nuts."

Me: "Anyway, what the hell was I going to do with two drunken sluts anyway?"

A: "Yeah, what would anyone possibly do in a situation like that?"

B: "You wouldn't go, either."

A: "Bullshit. I would be all up in that."

B: "Whatever."

A: "You would go."

Me: "It doesn't matter. I wasn't invited."

A: "Until next time."

B: "I would not go home with two lesbians I met at a party at someone named Chirpy's house."

A: "You're such a liar."

Me: "They were bisexual. Anyway, I wasn't invited."

B: "There's no such thing. You are either one or the other."

A: "We're not getting into this again."

Me: "They won't even remember me, I'm sure."

B: "But you're the magnet!"

Me: "All right move over. I'm driving. There's a bus. Let him out to catch a ride home and I'm going to drive us into it."

A: "Let's go back and get Chirpy."

XV

My hands were red and cracked and I, out of utter irritation, was drumming the railing surrounding my porch. I could no longer feel my nose or ears. I couldn't feel them by touch, but I was aware of the stinging hurt of bitter cold that now seared them.

I wasn't moving from that porch and I had two good reasons not to do so: I needed to see her car as soon as possible so as not to waste any more time with her getting there, getting out, coming up to the door, knocking on the door, coming in, probably needing to go to the bathroom or fix her makeup, maybe needing to get a drink...no, I needed to be outside to interrupt that process and force the progression of the wasting night. Secondly, she needed to see as soon as she possibly could that I was pissed.

I tried in vain to remember the shape of her headlights, so I would know before seeing the car itself if it were her. The house was on the corner of three streets, but the two behind me were one way and so the direction I was facing had been decided for me.

I was wearing a bright blue sequin shirt under a black jacket that I refused to zip up all the way, no matter how damn cold I got. The fabric of the jacket not warmed by my body was frigid, and I took great care not to move so that it wouldn't meet skin it had not already met. In my state of literal frozen animation, I was much like a Christmas tree adorned with gleaming plastic icicles that were set twinkling by the oncoming headlights. She would see me.

It was the shirt, in fact, that was the indirect cause for our tardiness as she put it, though I saw her selfishness as the lone obstacle standing between me and the sheer awe-inspiring delight of aural overwhelming that was the show we were now missing.

I would be noticed in this shirt and I knew that my hero had one similar (in silver, long-sleeved) that he might be wearing tonight. I let my mind construct a ridiculous, yet plausible scene where I would be applauded for my shimmer and maybe, just maybe, consequently receive an invitation to trade notes and anecdotes in the bus or backstage. I pushed the pleasantness of the reverie out of my head and focused on being livid.

She would not allow the balance of attention to shift my way and her lack of self-assurance forced her to seek out a worthy nemesis for my ensemble.

The search began earlier that day and led us to a series of mythical thrift stores nearly an hour outside of the city. It was rumored that in the rows of musty racks lie the treasures of days gone by, when fashion was powerful, and its edges framed the now absent class and character of an entire society. The fable was lent legitimacy by a portrait of the surrounding town—once wealthy, now left barren by the exodus of industry and those who drove it. All that remained were the drones living off miscellaneous "settlements" from the companies, neighbors, and failed relationships that fell victim to whatever misfortune they now suffered; the drones and the clothes of rich old people who had left them behind. The remaining inhabitants knew nothing of style and so even though the stores were frequently visited, the goods of interest to us stood unstirred on their hangers.

Unlike the grand city of gold swallowed by the sea or fountain that assured eternal youth, these destinations were themselves easily located. But, with them we also found great disappointment. I tried to remain objective and account for the exaggeration of word of mouth communication, but the bounty still fell far short of my dulled expectations, failing even to produce the one jewel that could have salvaged the journey and preclude my assignment to the cold front porch. As such, she didn't have a thing to wear.

She was beautiful and truly needed no garnishing to warrant focus from the room, but the proclamation of it seemed only like a rushed attempt to catch what remained of the second opening act (we had determined that we missed the first before she left for home, 35 minutes away, to change into an as-of-yet undecided ensemble of her own).

And so, I stood.

There was no wind and so it was the encompassing, still cold of a walk-in freezer. My hands had stopped moving despite the growing state of my frustration. The thick wax in the arching mound of hair atop my head was hard from the cold and served well at this temperature its purpose of staying vertical. I wouldn't be needing the novelty switchblade comb in my pocket until some time had passed in the close heat of the club, if we ever made it there.

I was trying my best to pose in the dismissive, yet discontent stance of a traditional greaser while ignoring the occasional mocking snicker of passersby. I was my own version of cool and the version of cool I thought was shared by those I idolized and imitated. It wasn't supposed to matter what anyone else thought—anyone, that is, that wouldn't be at this show or with similar people at a similar one somewhere else. Putting myself on display to be the subject of ridicule by the squares in my dirty neighborhood only made me angrier at her for extending the exhibit.

There were so many good reasons to go inside, hide, and warm up, but to me, there were better to stay out. I hoped that she would mistake the cold-bitten redness of my cheeks for surfacing anger.

Roughly an hour and 18 minutes after leaving to change, the tiny headlights of her compact automobile grew as she approached. As suspected, she saw me from a distance and the pitch of the car whined as she pointlessly hurried the last hundred yards.

Her face was a wrenched competition between sincere apology and resentment of the impending scolding. I meant to pause for dramatic effect when the car skidded to halt, but I was already opening the door when it pushed the gravel and scattered tufts of crabgrass into piles underneath it.

She stuck her chin out and lowered her head like a dog with a history of abuse and didn't lean over to kiss me until a block later. She received cold, pursed lips when she did and, in response, tried fleetingly to turn my reaction into something she could be mad about, but it didn't take.

We didn't speak until well after pulling up to the back dock of the club where the show had ended minutes before. The conclusion was confirmed by someone I barely knew but yelled at from the car. As a slow turn of the wide, jagged knife in my side, they added that it was a great show, the best of his they had seen. I clenched my jaw and said not a word as I got back in the car and stared forward towards a night of vain, yet passionate reconciliation.

Nicholas J. Stevens

XVI

My mom was the house manager of the community theatre owned by the massive multinational corporation she worked for. Since it was owned by a massive multinational corporation, the bad actors in heavy makeup had a much nicer stage to stink on and a much larger audience to do it in front of.

The theatre itself was enormous and was housed entirely within one of the buildings that defined the company's world headquarters. I spent my weekends as an usher in the balcony and made my mom brand me with the meaningless title of Balcony Manager.

There were two staircases that led to the balcony, each were approximately 10 feet wide and the equivalent of about four normal stories high. The balcony itself was divided into four sections, each with 16 rows. The middle section was a uniform 24 seats across in every row, but the two ancillary sections started at half as many seats at the top and came to a point in the front row, which had only two seats. No one ever sat in those front two seats except me and maybe a friend or cousin I could sucker into joining me for the night.

I was also in charge in filling up the small, wax paper cups from two-litre bottles of soda in preparation for intermission. This earned me the additional meaningless title of concessions manager. The bottles and ice were up in a room several floors above the arcade area where the tables stood to sell drinks and candy bars. I recalled being excited by the word "ARCADE" perched atop the doorway on the street when I was too young to know that it was just the sloping walkway between the two bustling avenues on each side. Disappointment fell heavy on me the first night I accompanied my mother with a pocket full of quarters, they are being fated only to free a bag of nacho cheese snacks and not to activate a joystick or my delight.

The excitement of unsupervised exploration in an old theatre, not to mention the surrounding enormity of the office building, was enough to keep me occupied when I had company, but it wasn't as much fun to shoot the bows and arrows from Peter Pan at the Styrofoam heads in the costume room when I was by myself. Since the shows ran late, any friend of mine that I invited would have to stay the night and that was sometimes more of an event than was allowed by their parents. A few times I had multiple friends or a friend and a cousin and we could play cards using the sugar-rich sodas for drinking games. This made for an unruly sleepover, but once the sugar was spent and we deflated, we were dead to the world.

At three days per weekend during seasons that could run over a month, there were inevitably shifts where no friends could be found. I would wander the halls and sit at the end of stretching desks in empty boardrooms, spinning around in the big leather chairs and talking to myself. Sometimes I would push grainy colored lines across the dry erase boards on the walls, only to reduce them to smudges on the ends of my fingers. Rarely, but enough to memorize every line, I would sit at one of the lone front seats on the sides of the balcony and watch the performances.

I had to fetch ice and fill cups, so I never saw the scenes before intermission, and I had to clean up, so I never saw the ones right after. It didn't really matter to me and I only watched what I watched when there was nothing else I could light on fire, rearrange, or leave my mark on.

The only variations, aside from the shows themselves and the occasional forgotten line, were the volunteer ushers. They were

Nicholas J. Stevens

also family and friends of people who worked there or friends of friends or family of family. There were also a number of those who had appeared in shows previously and enjoyed still being a little behind the scenes, while helping the theatre at the same time. This produced more people my age and, though not often, a romantic interest that wasn't heavily made up, several hundred feet away, and much less interesting in the yellow lights of the lobby during the reception after the show.

As Balcony Manager, I gave detailed instructions to the volunteers: teaching them how the seats and sections were numbered, how to read the tickets, and in general what to do in whatever situation one might encounter while leading old people and the culturally deficient to their seats. I was good at it and enjoyed overseeing and guiding people who, under any other circumstance, would have been my uncle, peer, teacher, ex-girlfriend, or any role of better in the social hierarchy.

Tonight, I was given an abnormally large crew of five ushers, no less than four of whom were my own age. Three were of little-to-no interest to me and the other was a crown of blonde curls atop a pale, slight frame.

Her name was Lillie and she answered my query by stating that she had been in the last production of *Babes in Toyland*, the same one that marked the commencement and conclusion of my sister's grand career as a thespian. She had a minor role as a soldier and something else, but I didn't remember her and wouldn't have recognized her without the ridiculous hat and red circles painted on her face. My mother kept at least one copy of all the programs and I would have to look her up when I got home.

Since there were two staircases leading up to the balcony, both required staffing with ushers. Since I was in charge and since

I was pretty sure that she wanted to become more acquainted, I assigned her, myself, and her round-headed friend, Charlie, to the near set of stairs. The other two and one of the townspeople's neighbor or something were cast off to the far staircase until after the curtain rose.

When it did, I allowed them to have a seat and volunteered myself to stay and round up the stragglers. It was easier for me anyway since I knew the sections and rows like the back of my shaky hand and wouldn't have to distract anyone by using the flashlight. Lillie insisted that I sit with them and watch the show when I was finished, and I agreed just as the thought struck me that, given their dilettante seating abilities, I might accidentally be rubbing elbows with Charlie and his round head.

My fears were quickly laid to rest as I stepped down and saw Lillie in B16 seat 23, saving the B16, seat 24 for me. She smiled at me when I sat and put her hand on my arm to settle me into my seat. It was a very theatric gesture and wafted of a southern belle she had probably played at some point in a school production. She had touched me and so it was already way better than lighting spray glitter paint on fire in the prop room.

Most of the people in attendance had paid good money (more than double the going price for an evening cinema ticket) to see the show, so if we were to speak at all, it had to be at or below a whisper. This was conducive to being within personal space boundaries it would have taken me several outings to cross on my own.

When she spoke, the air of her words ran across the tiny hairs that rimmed my outer ear, sending a shiver and wave of euphoria over me. I had only ever kissed one girl and she was my girlfriend of a middle school eternity of just over three months. Lillie, with her pretend blonde curls and red lipstick, sought to graduate me into a level of intimacy I had yet to experience.

Without even the illusion of control, my eyes fell half shut with every descent from the hiss of whisper to the low hum of hidden speech that her voice took. My mind averted the possibilities by reminding me of the hazards of cheap, smearable lipstick and that I should pay closer attention to balancing the program I cleverly stored on my lap.

The blood in my head was beating frantically on the wall of my eardrum like a prisoner who had forgotten the futility of flesh against concrete. I couldn't hear a word she was saying but was lulled into divinity by the encompassing tones of her syntax.

My head turned toward her, and I could make out enough of her face in the streaks of illumination that escaped from the side of the spotlight above us to see that she was smiling at me. She was lovely, and I was petrified with nerves.

She leaned in and kissed me on the mouth. She inched back, and I returned the lean and kissed her.

Later, outside of the coatroom downstairs, Charley informed me that she was a good girl and a good friend of his and that I shouldn't hurt her. It was more chivalrous than threatening and I applauded the sense of necessity bred by his friendship. It also made me suspect that he secretly wanted her to be hurt as an opportunity to divulge a crush of his own that he may or may not ever tell her about.

XVII

Jim Smooth, who wasn't, and I put on suits to go to a swing show. The only other time we had an opportunity to wear suits was when we acted on rumors of a swing dance night held in the ballroom of the mammoth hotel in the heart of downtown. An amused desk clerk informed us that we were several months too late. Disheartened, we spotted a well-dressed couple and an old man holding a shiny, pink box and followed them up to what turned out to be a wedding reception on one of the private floors much higher up.

We smiled a lot in the elevator even though none of the other passengers were looking at us and we telepathically agreed to remain in silence so as not to blow our cover. When the mirrored doors split, I held my plaid arm out to keep Jim back a step behind the others. We floated around the entrance to the grand ballroom, trying to convince ourselves that no one would notice or question our presence there, but every caught eye from the dance floor stunned us in nervous immobility.

There was no possible way that anyone in the literal hundreds of attendees that made up the cast of the revelry would ever know or care that we were not on the imagined "list." This point we concurred as we walked about outside around the dark streets of a vacant downtown, still fresh in our suits and eager for another party we would not attend and an opportunity to redeem ourselves we would not seize.

Nicholas J. Stevens

The show was open to big band enthusiasts of all ages, but most of those over 21 would not attend a function without at least the possibility of cocktails. The promoters had this in mind when they chose this venue, There was a bar that ran parallel to the stage about 80 feet back, encased in a chain link fence that climbed up to the high ceiling above it. Much like those that jogged the perimeter of baseball fields, it had only one narrow opening and this one was filled with the shoulders of a man whose purpose it was to keep out underage boys and underage, unattractive girls.

Like the special agents in movies, I took immediate and specific inventory of everyone in the room upon entering it. I paused under the glowing red exit sign to get a clear and panoramic view and to imagine that heads were turning to admire me and my suit. Jim bumped me and chortled in confusion, questioning my posed hesitation.

I liked to pretend that he was an apprentice as well as my friend and often narrated my actions to him as I moved. As to what exactly I was supposed to be edifying him in, I'm not sure, but I had on a better jacket and my tie was thinner, so I did it anyway.

It was a cornucopia of interests and they were all done up perfectly—saddle shoes and vintage dresses; piled, twisted hair; lipstick; knotted, gossamer scarves; and the compulsory look of boredom that accompanied the subculture. It was heaven and the angels wore real nice skirts.

I had logged at least a half dozen girls I would ignore for the remainder of the night to obtain their interest and I had done so out loud as if Jim were taking a memo. He agreed with my selections and added a few more that I had somehow overlooked, and I resolved in my head to let him have them since he had discovered them instead of me.

I gave a cool nod and a wink to some people I knew from work through the cross-hatching of the metal fence. They all laughed and a few tossed back shots of brightly-colored liquor from small, plastic cups. I knew that they would come out when the headlining band emerged but had no intention of leaving the comfort of proofed beverages to mingle with kids.

Jim was approached by a few girls he knew from wherever, but they were not in my mental library, so I diverted my attention after the introductions. They concluded their interlude quickly and I suggested that we make our way across the patch of parquet floor in front of the stage. It was a safe move this early in the intermission because the band wouldn't suddenly appear and strike up, stranding me in the tsunami of approaching swing kids and forcing me to jump and bop. Despite looking the part, I danced like a washing machine filled with wet bedding and took great care to not make this fact known.

After several minutes of scanning the room just ahead of return glances, the band sauntered on stage to the cheers and whistles of the growing crowd. They warmed up briefly with a cacophony of colliding notes and then the thick mass of a trumpet player drowned out all others with a rich squeal. It was shrill and hypnotic, like getting mysteriously inured to an incessant smoke alarm.

And he blew.

He laid out the one stinging note as a blanket on which the others were to settle and open baskets and pouches of goods to enjoy. The drummer rattled in, rising and falling and resting in the rhythmic interruptions of a tight drum skin between tinkling cymbal ticks. Another horn came in in a rapid swirl of notes, an inviting contrast to the single note still being held by the stiffly inflated head atop the hulking shirt and tie.

The crooner in charge was greeting them with a flurry of nicknames and pausing to allow for a cursory justification of their talents. All the while, the trumpet player blew. One note, for what seemed like an eternity as the suave voice presented the entire band. At the base of the gleaming brass curves, his face had taken the shape of forced roundness, like blown glass, and I imagined that it would either deflate and leave sliding flaps of stretched skin on either side of his head or stay hardened as globes beneath his eyes.

They leapt into one of their liveliest tunes and everyone roared. In my trance watching and listening to the siren of the trumpet, I hadn't noticed that my colleagues had evacuated the bar and spread out across the crowd. Derek was only a few feet from me and had grabbed a girl I knew from some class or another and began tossing her about. He was quite lively and a hell of a dancer, but his interest in women was only as something to lead on the dance floor.

He motioned to me and I gave what might have seemed to be a modestly reluctant refusal, but he insisted, and, after a brief and unnecessary introduction, he handed the girl off to me. I had no interest in her at all and was more unenthusiastic about the jig since it might jeopardize my chances with someone I was interested in if they saw me dance. We became locked in an awkward exchange of drawing near and then retreating continuously while switching back and forth to either sides of the other's head. The routine lasted way too long, and I managed a toothless smile and excused myself, still mid-song.

When I turned around, I did so into Benny's enormous grin. She was also part of the previously fenced-in bar crowd and the object of an ongoing crush I had since before taking up employment in the restaurant where we now all worked. We had gone out once to a haunted warehouse the previous Halloween and she had stayed the night in my childish loft bed. We had kissed and intertwined, but it was a stand-up double in sporting terms—no need to slide, though I don't think I would have been thrown out at third had I tried.

She was about a decade older than I, but of a young spirit and I liked her very much. I never expected a relationship or that we would go out again, just the two of us, but I knew that she liked me as well. She made it a point to enjoy life and its moments and in that way you could both appreciate her and fully understand that she couldn't do it within the confines of a relationship. It was the same way that animals in zoos aren't as fun or exhilarating as the images of them in their habitat, guided by instinct.

Her smile grew even wider when she realized it was me in front of her. She let out an undetectably high squeal as her shoulders rose up towards her ears. She put her hands on the sides of my pomade-slathered head and put her enormous mouth on mine. It felt as if she would swallow the entirety of me as her lips searched the perimeter of my smile and her tongue filled my mouth. She stepped back and stared at me with full moon eyes and then turned and grabbed Derek and led him to lead while she dramatically twisted, and I stood idle, too in awe to close my mouth or to reach for my comb.

Nicholas J. Stevens

XVIII

I sat next to Betty and ordered another gin and tonic from Paris. Not the city, Paris. She was the 19-year-old, well-intentioned but poorly trained bartender on duty that evening. I ordered another whatever with whiskey in it for Betty and we continued our introductions and easy beginning.

She was a pinup girl without a calendar or bomber plane behind her and I stared into her sleepy blue eyes as she talked, peering over the rim of my drink into the break of her shirt whenever I could.

She had on turquoise eye shadow and lip gloss the color of the gum inside lollipops. Her hair was the fitting bright blonde that moves in brighter waves when not restrained in a gathering behind her head, which it was.

I had seen her a few times walking about town and I am pretty sure she held a waitress position at the breakfast place right off campus or did at one point. I caught her sleepy eye once walking by the long window in front and resigned from that point on to always look in and step a little slower past.

It was one of those looks that you certainly notice but is so brief and potentially inconsequential that you're never really sure if the other person noticed it. I was planning on posing the inquiry after the next sip and peep and was preparing myself for either confirmation or outright confusion, when she beat me to it and posed a similar question of her own.

She was one of the incoming freshmen I oversaw during their testing sessions the summer before they began college. I had run out of money that same summer and did not return in the fall but remained good friends with some of the kids I met and ran about town with them when I could. At times I felt a little pathetic to be hanging around with a clan of freshmen while not even attending the school and being a year ahead if I had.

It was a misguided notion as most of them were the same age as I and some were even older. The origin of the stratification was the perceived hierarchy of grade levels (or "years" as they referred to them in the realm of higher education) as well as the fact that I was of some authority while they were at their testing sessions.

She asked if I remembered her from her session and I convinced myself almost instantly that I did. I think I did. No, I did. She hung out with that red-haired girl and that kid with the gargantuan, impractically white coat. Was it her or was I cutting and pasting her image into a vague assembly of background characters? It didn't matter, and I told her I did and even mentioned the kid with the white coat to add a detail of believability. I thought that it would serve as a subliminal seed that would grow into a memory that she didn't experience if I was wrong about it being her.

I wasn't sure as to how it was going and was struggling with whether or not I would excuse myself and go into the other room to watch the rather colorful band rock it up.

They were clad in Fred Flintstone-style, one-piece, animal print costumes, complete with the wildly jagged cut on the bottom. They were playing respectively themed instruments and the drummer was beating on large kettle drums with two oversized femur bones. On a normal night, they would have easily captured and retained my attention, but I felt more like sitting and Betty had much better legs.

Without turning back towards me completely, Betty said, "Let's go," as nonchalantly as a seasoned robber watching unsuspecting guards exit an armored truck at precisely the calculated time.

She lived only a half mile or so from the bar, but it was an impressive distance in heels and we walked the whole way. We went in and I gave a guilty and uncomfortable wave to her roommates while she gathered, among other things, her car keys.

It was not a good idea to be driving in her condition and an even worse idea to be riding along. I converted my mind to the idea that we would inevitably be taking the "back way" under the bridge and would doubtfully encounter any other cars. I forced out the obvious logic that the only other cars that we might encounter would be other intoxicated automobile operators also trying to avoid traffic and arrest.

We joined quickly inside the heavy door of my apartment. There was no tour, no offers to make herself comfortable, no offer of tea or juice. Her lip gloss quickly, and with great force, encircled my mouth. Her hands were stuck in the thick wax of my once-coiffed hair and she pushed me back onto the couch.

Astride and teetering over me, a collision with the coffee table knocked off one of her shoes and I was aware that she noticed not at all. My hands were running the smooth length of the back of her legs under her skirt and I attempted to pause momentarily for air...to no avail.

Almost as suddenly as it had begun, she stopped.

"Let's go back to my place," she said.

This was, of course, acceptable, but confusing, since we had only moments before left her place to come here. I had assumed that she was gathering brushes of sorts and tubes of necessities, though I hadn't noticed until now that her small handbag was nowhere to be seen along the short trail from the door to the love seat.

I chose not to mirror this collecting of toiletries for both the reasons that I was anxious to resume the engagement, and, after the previous change of venue, I wasn't sure that we would actually be staying there for any length of time. Also, I thought it was kind of cool if a girl let you use her toothbrush or if you let one use yours; it seemed to me even more intimate than kissing.

I greeted her roommates with another half wave and this time made my way past them into her bedroom. She pushed me to one side, near her bed, but did not follow and instead stayed across the room near the red chest of drawers under the mirror.

She reached in the second drawer from the top and emerged with a fistful of leopard print, a very similar pattern to the bass player from the band back at the bar. She instructed me to cover my eyes and began wiggling out of her skirt while still facing me. I playfully put my hands to my cheeks while splitting my fingers wide apart to peek through. She gave me a quick scolding glance and proceeded to pull off the shirt I so contently peered into not hours before.

The lights were still very much on and I could see that she had on the same print, though more gossamer and comprised of much less fabric, underneath the new layer she was putting on. This was obviously a special outfit and I was flattered to be the catalyst for its appearance. I was also relieved that it came from the chest of drawers and not the hamper.

The ensemble was that of a crushed velour camisole and boy shorts and it felt as if you could rub your name in it if you went against the grain. I was on my back on the bed and again she opted to tower over me and drench with me looks she thought to be seductive. It was charming, but unnecessary to seduce someone already underneath the weight of a leopard-skinned assembly of curves. My mouth could not find the means to make jest of the objectively comic behavior, so I just smiled and stretched my lips to whatever I could when it came near.

The special attire had made its way to the floor without her and it was she who was now splayed facing upwards towards the ceiling. I was not over her and she could only see my comically seductive looks if she lifted her head from its resting place on the pillow.

Moments and minutes passed and soon I wondered if the frozen state of bliss I imagined she was in was not immobility by another means. I tested my theory by first whispering her name with the caution of a young adult swearing to his parents for the first time. There was no response.

I said it again and pushed down on my elbows, arching my back enough to see her fallen head and blonde locks scattering from her face in all directions. I repeated her name again, this time with a question mark at the end of it and with greater volume. There was no response.

I sat up and looked over the breadth of her skin while trying with conviction to shove a chair under the doorknob of my mind, keeping out those thoughts that conscience would have no trouble with were it not for gin.

No physical manifestation of a demon appeared on my shoulder, but unscrupulous suggestions hinted that, were she among the conscious, she would not only not object to my actions, but that it would undoubtedly be me who would cease the proceedings before any personal promises were broken. It was a useless argument and the imp at my ear would again know defeat.

I collapsed to her side and pulled the sheet up over us and gave her one last, lingering kiss, this time on her forehead.

Nicholas J. Stevens

XIX

I thought we were just going to be playing the piano. I mean, her mom was in the kitchen only 10 or so yards from us. Sharing a narrow piano bench was plenty exciting enough for me. I was already content.

Marilyn was sultry. She had long, wavy, light auburn hair and full lips. She wasn't beautiful by the standards she hoped to fulfill, like in the magazines she read religiously. But she carried herself with a sensuality far beyond my 10th grade level. Plus, I skipped a grade, so I was way out of my league in the presence of her revved-up motor.

She was showing me how to play *The Godfather* theme, or at least part of it, over and over. I was concentrating intently on the keys, occasionally slowing to a trickle to add a sense of drama and weight. I had never played an instrument and the closest thing to musical involvement was a dance class my mother had signed me up for in grade school, which isn't close at all.

She would occasionally lace her arm between mine and play the keys flanked by mine. This brought us physically very close together and she would look up as if to verify my understanding of a point or lesson, bringing us only inches away from touching at least noses.

I was already not that good at playing the piano, so my mistakes seemed understandable as a lack of skill. The truth was that I was so incredibly nervous, I could have been an adolescent Tchaikovsky and my voice still would have cracked, and my hands still would have fumbled like a child returned from a sled-riding marathon. I heard no notes and could think of nothing other than our mouths pressing together and her mother in the other room.

***

Marilyn came over to my house a week or so later. I don't know if it was due to my parents wanting to watch a program on the family television or because they trusted me, but they let Marilyn ascend to my room unchaperoned.

The thought entered my mind that my mom's trust was boosted by her high regard for her heightened skills of perception. One night, I was watching a program she had banned because of its late air time and she had collared me when she followed a suspicion and came up to check on me. She laid her hand across the top of the television, felt its warmth (because I had quickly and with great paranoia just snapped it off), and declared that I wasn't fooling anyone and was grounded.

I was pretty sure at least somewhere in her mind she took this into account when she allowed Marilyn to come up, thinking that if anything needed discovery and discipline, she would discover it and administer the discipline.

Marilyn was slowly pacing around my room, picking up the memorabilia (only worthy of remembrance to a child whose procrastination was delaying maturity) and wiping the dust on her jeans. I was sitting cross-legged on the AstroTurf, playing a video game about remote-controlled racing cars. The AstroTurf was the durable, yet uncomfortable result of me convincing my parents to further support my soccer career and line my room with it.

The indirect attention I was paying to Marilyn was a mix of nerves and puberty. The nervousness was fueling my overly good behavior, accompanied by an excessive respect I thought was chivalrous. Marilyn found it tedious. I thought I was being a gentleman, but I think she saw it as a challenge.

Nicholas J. Stevens

I was still playing and answering her questions while staying locked on the screen when she walked in front of me, stepped forward, and lowered to make a tight-jeaned, curvy canopy straddling me.

I dropped my controller, put my mouth on hers and my hands on her sides, then her back, and immediately grew up.

I had several other things much more important on my mind, so I wasn't worrying about my mother or her detective prowess. Besides, I assumed that if Marilyn was confident enough to take the step she and we were taking, she had a plan to avoid discovery or apprehension.

We sat braided in a huddled mass of teenage passion, stopping only for juice and air. Under the guidance of her unspoken words, I moved my hands over her, carefully avoiding territory that could have resulted in devastating embarrassment if not endorsed and desired. Her movements and whispered words guided me, and she was pleased with her manipulation. I could feel her lips changing into the smile of a mission accomplished.

When she eventually left, my parents were polite and told Marilyn she was welcome to come back any time. I emphasized this, then scampered back up to my room to note on my Winnie the Pooh calendar the date of my first trip to second base. With still-shaking hands, I crudely drew two stars in red ink, beaming as I did.

L (part 1)

"What the fuck is this?"

Violet confronted me in what was declared as our "study." There was a desk with a computer atop it; two comfortable, old, red chairs that looked essential in a room called a "study" that whispered to have the books on the walls read in them; a rug that almost spanned the area of the room; a silver-haired, beautiful woman with rage in her eyes; and me, a man dumbfounded by the impetus for her rage, though not at all by the rage itself. She was armed with ammunition that was not intended to be used as such and had not been shown to her intentionally.

"..."

"WHAT THE FUCK IS THIS?"

"It's something I was writing. Well, something I am writing."

"WHAT THE FUCK IS THIS?!?"

"It's a book about kisses. It's an homage to..."

"What? What the fuck? Kisses?!? What the fuck is this?"

Our discussion, which could only loosely be described as such, went on like this in a timeless vacuum. I repeatedly attempted to explain that the book—the collection and documentation of every woman I had ever kissed on the mouth—was intended to be an homage to her. It was to honor her as the one I chose to be the only one I would ever kiss ever again. The others, good, bad, or terrible, made the man who was her husband.

I knew there was a better chance of it being accepted—possibly even appreciated, though doubtfully ever endorsed—if I kept it a secret until it was finished. Her lack of trust and knowledge of computers, along with spyware and my regrettable decision to send some of it via email to Will—who I had never kissed but was a character in several of the chapters—made it a moot point. She prematurely found what I had written and reacted.

To be continued...

XX

Penelope instructed me to "wait a second," then floated back into the room on a scooter. Not a motorized vehicle, but one of those scooters that consisted of a thin skateboard with a steering post attached to it. This one also had a bell.

It was also embellished with colorful streamers, glitter, shiny metallic stickers, and the charm of her effervescent spirit. The enormous smile she wore atop it was framed by a subtly blushing face, which was giant enough to dwarf the smile. The stark boldness of her toothy grin was reminiscent of the hood ornaments worn by automobiles when size and aerodynamics were of little to no interest.

I shared how impressed and envious I was as she proudly circled. She explained that an ex-boyfriend, who shared my name and was still a major part of her life from a distance, had preened it for her in the twilight of their relationship before she left for school.

Penelope was vibrant, beautiful, and bursting with life and the youth it grew from. She was a year under me in school (a freshman) and I was drawn to her ardor for the simplest things, like glittery scooters and sticker books. I had found an old sticker book when new friends and I went exploring on neighborhood trash night. I had once showed it off to Penelope and she bounced with excitement and appreciation.

She was shorter than me and had long, straight blonde hair she kept clean and orderly. She was in remarkably, almost questionably good shape and I realized not long before that I might have been the only one in my circle of male friends whose remarks were innocent and G-rated in nature. I was in good shape, too, but I had to work at it. Her lines and edges were more defined and pronounced, but she said it was "just natural, I guess."

Her physique was highlighted by her clothes. Rarely did her shirts have sleeves and even less often did they join her loosely belted trousers. They were associates, in that they were familiar with each other, but would quickly separate when she threw her hands up in celebration of things few others would take enjoyment from.

Male friends and acquaintances would go into unsettling detail about things they wanted her to do and things they would do to and with her. I would agree that she was striking but refused to partake in the hypothetical robbing of her innocence. Maybe it was her childlike zeal, but I felt the need to protect her from the vultures who high-five or smell fingers after their real or imagined sexual conquests.

As we sat on her couch, with only the light from the television illuminating the room, I was very glad to have a front row seat to the exhibition of her smile. Without explanation or consequent investigation, she was also very tan, and it made her grin jump out even more. I kissed her, with no intention behind it other than more kisses. I liked kissing and it was becoming clearer to me that kissing to most people was a precursor to more intimate things. I hoped she felt comfortable and safe and didn't see me as a jackal foraging for more. I was reassured by the smile stretching across the breadth of her enormous face each time we broke and leaned back for air or to relish in it.

"Do you want to see mine?" she asked with an eagerness that both excited me and made me a bit nervous. Instantly, I reasoned to myself how doubtful it was that she would ask or suggest anything I should be afraid of.

"Okay. Do I want to see your what?" I was smiling, too, with a foundation of confusion and skepticism underneath.

"My sticker book!"

We hadn't been talking about my sticker book or the sticker books of others or even the basic concept of the theoretical sticker book. It further cemented my belief that she was a good, simple person.

I nodded, smiling, and I gave her naked shoulder a squeeze.

"I would love to."

XXI

"So, what do I do? What's the thing I'm supposed to do?"

I was pretending to seek edification regarding a pinball machine I had played countless times and at great length. Some of the times I had repeatedly played this machine were when I accompanied a friend with rolls of quarters my dad had sent me in the mail. She had once been honored with the title of Women's MVP of the Steel City Pinball Association. The World Championships (yeah, of pinball) were held in the Steel City of Pittsburgh, Pennsylvania and she was the Most Valuable Player of the league. I tried to keep up and learn what I could, and I brought quarters my dad sent me. She smiled at that. She only needed a few of them and won the rest of her games, and some of mine as well.

Tonight, I was pretending to not know and only vaguely understand the finer points of the game. I was also failing to complete the tasks I did understand. That is, until the topic of "making it interesting" was brought up.

He was already several more drinks into the evening and I knew I wasn't yet intoxicated. I could tell by the spent fruit count at the bottom of my plastic cup. This establishment made a habit of not giving new cups (and never glasses) for new drinks of the same kinds. I was drinking gins and tonics, and, by the lime wedge count, I only had two.

We agreed to play for drinks, but my desire to win was fueled by ego and not a desire to be inebriated on someone else's dime. I was submerged in the rockabilly/greaser subculture and had a strong affinity for very publicly playing the part. I was pretty sure that hustling someone at pinball for gins and tonics earned me cool points from those with better boots, tighter cuffs, and higher pompadours. I had a strong, but misguided feeling it would result in increased attention from the dollies in the room, too. Maybe I was tipsier than I realized.

There was a band playing in the other room and although they were not my focus, I did want to see them. I was not of legal drinking age and considered every song heard or drink enjoyed a stolen opportunity from the authorities, whoever they were. The lead guitarist/vocalist was of some stature at the bar. Maybe I heard he was the owner or part owner or something important, but tonight he was the entertainment.

I was done mopping up the fetid, sticky floor with the poor sap who challenged me to one of my favorite pins. Now I just wanted to have refreshing beverages, play a few more games of non-competitive pinball, and listen to music that would make me tap a foot, maybe two.

Women were present, and I wanted their attention, as I always did, but I was not putting forth any real effort to develop anything. I just wanted to show off my hair, pretend to not care about it at all, and play some pinball. I didn't even know there was going to be a band, let alone the owner (or whoever)'s band, but maybe I had heard of them and maybe I got word they were good stuff.

At one point during the show, they were performing a cover of a classic tune, a real staple of any rockabilly disciple, and the singer forgot the words to a verse. I was certain he knew it and simply couldn't bring it to the forefront of his mind, but he publicly sought assistance with the words before repeating the lines from an earlier verse.

Oh, I was mad at myself! I knew the verse and every word in it and all the words in the verses that bookended it! I knew it but was too nervous to speak up! I desperately tried to convince myself that my silence was due to my age and desire to remain undetected by authority, but I couldn't ignore the reality that I was just scared.

The band played on and as they did, I scanned the crowd for familiar faces and faces I wouldn't mind being familiar with. All the men looked personally invested in every word and chord and fired up by them. All the women appeared to be in a competition to be the most unenthused in attendance and most appeared to be simply tolerating the show. Yep, it was a rockabilly show at a rockabilly bar.

Among the dispassionate faces and their shiny red lips was Doris. She was aesthetically classic—house dress, female pompadour, cherry lips, curvaceous build, all of it. She looked beautiful, extremely bored, and moderately annoyed watching her beau thrilling the rest of the crowd. She was (allegedly) going steady with the front man of the band. He was such a mystery! Maybe he was the owner? Maybe he was Doris' fella? Maybe he knew the words to "Rockabilly Boogie?" I would've liked answers, but certainly didn't need them.

Doris was friends with a couple of the older girls who made it their business to learn me the ropes. They steered me clear of and warned me about a girl affectionately christened "Hatchet Face." I could've probably figured that one out on my own, but I still appreciated it.

When she saw me, Doris nodded subtly, and I returned the gesture with a reverse nod where I tilted my chin up an inch or two. The downward nod seemed to me to be a sign of acknowledgement, but the kind of thing someone did before a gunfight. Not that I took Doris' nod as a warning of her intent to shoot me, it just felt different when a woman did it. I couldn't explain it if asked, but luckily no one ever did.

I didn't know how old Doris was and wasn't bold enough to ask. She was out of my league in many ways, so inquiring about her years on the same planet as me wouldn't serve any productive purpose. I had gone on a few dates with women whose ages didn't end in "teen," though mine did. I wasn't nervous then and even had an actual girlfriend who was 25 when I was 19. It only bothered me when I was pretending to know stuff that I would only begin to comprehend years from then and she would talk down to me. It didn't happen often, and she was probably just trying to keep my arrogance in check, but it irked me.

"I thought you were already gone," said Doris when she sauntered over and greeted me, expressionless.

"No, I'm still here. Not much longer, but...still here now," I said. I was nervous now. I don't know if she had that effect on everyone, though I thought she certainly did. "And, I wanted to come in and say goodbye to people I may not see if I stop in again."

If I was outside myself and heard me talking, I was pretty sure I would declare me an idiot. But I wasn't outside myself and thought I was being pretty smooth...sort of. A quick glance in my plastic cup revealed at least five crushed and spent lime wedges, but I didn't think they had anything to do with my charm.

Still without any visual insight into her emotions, Doris said, "Well, if I don't see you, good luck."

She leaned in and kissed me, right on the mouth.

I couldn't hear the music over the sound of blood pumping through my brain and chest, but the kiss was one beat longer than a polite well-wishing. It was still short enough and administered with closed mouths to avoid a brawl with all the greasers in the room, including the lead singer who may or may not be her fella.

I exhaled slow as she turned, poised and with perfect posture, and carried her curves back to her station and exaggerated boredom. Without wiping my lips, I went back to playing pinball and trying to reel in another sap to add to my lime collection.

XXII

My best friend was president of the National Honor Society and he could write hall passes whenever he wanted. He loved playing cards like I loved playing cards and he used his status to establish competitive foursomes for card games. Scandalous? Perhaps. But the only fun that could be had in the cafeteria study hall was saying the word "scrotum" louder and louder with your tablemates until the bravest (and loudest) got detention.

He wrote hall passes for me and Barbara and a few others, so we could play Euchre together in the chemical room of the chemistry class. It can be a confusing game, and I didn't understand a lick of it before I spent a whole summer at Noah's house and the first several weeks of the school year getting comfortable with it. Now I understood the intricacies and was a formidable opponent in competitive situations.

I would've won the card tournament the aforementioned best friend held at his house, but Barbara had to be home before the tournament concluded. It was a round robin style thing where everybody played at least once with everybody else. I let the host's little brother sit in for me while I returned my girlfriend home before her offensively early curfew.

When I left, I was winning. My substitute need only be competent, which he swore he was, to keep me in the lead and in a position to win money. It wasn't much but was more than I got for at least one of my jobs, refereeing little kids' soccer games. It would probably even be more than I got for painting faces at fairs and company picnics; maybe not—painting faces at fairs and company picnics pays surprisingly well.

It didn't matter because when I returned, I was losing...badly. It had rather abruptly become what I referred to as a "washout night." On top of the world, beating all my friends and exchanging glances across the felt with my lovely girlfriend became losing at cards and spending the rest of the night explaining Euchre to my best friend's little brother. It was painfully obvious why he hadn't initially been allowed to play.

———

My best friend and two others were still gloating and offering patronizing fake sympathy a few days later when we struck up a new game in the chemistry room. My girlfriend was also a member of the Honor Society, so a note was often written for her and she would often play cards with us.

She was two years younger in school and it amused me that she had a very "sophomoric" sense of humor. I never told anyone that joke, and I doubt most would've gotten it if I had. Besides, I don't think my friends truly liked her and I didn't want to highlight more reasons to not do so. They were polite to her and extended invitations to her to anything I was invited to, but in terms of personality, she was an acquired taste.

Playing cards in the chemical room was fun and since it was not usually for money, it was even more fun. The part I looked forward to the most, however, was when the game was done. Everyone would push in their stools and gather their folders and the books they were supposed to be reading. The quarters were close, so it was a good idea to just slide past others to avoid knocking over caustic chemicals and the glass jars that held them captive.

Barbara and I used the close quarters to press our often-flannel-and-jean-covered bodies together for a brief second and share a kiss. She was already tall, but when she wore flannel, she wore boots, too, and it was an exciting and wonderful stretch up to kiss her.

The chemistry teacher, who was less polite to me than my friends were to my girlfriend, definitely didn't like me. I think it had something to do with my insecurity prohibiting me from taking the more advanced level of chemistry. She knew I was smart, and I think she was annoyed I wasn't challenging myself or living up to my potential—something parental. I probably reminded her of something she didn't like about one of her own kids.

She became outwardly annoyed, almost hostile, when she interrupted Barbara and I sharing an extended kiss and moving hands across each other. From that point on, we spent our study hall periods in the library. It was cleaner, quieter, and there were no (visible) harmful substances looming over us. We got booted out of there for a few days, too, due to an entirely different instance of exchanging smooches. We were also interrupted by the stark beam of a policeman's searchlight on another occasion, but it was much less embarrassing since he was in his car and we were in my parents' enormous sedan.

Still another time—and we never got pulled over because I had the cruise control keeping us at a mild 54 miles per hour—we had just come from a performance of a blockbuster animated film by real people on ice. It was not even ironically cool, but I agreed to go and was excited about it. I was in love. I would have still thought it was pretty lame if someone else had done it.

Things had not gotten very physical between us despite the appearance we projected. Sure, we got kicked out of everywhere for kissing, but physical intimacy was a big deal to both of us. Just agreeing verbally that we would give our innocence to the other was enough. We didn't feel the need to test it. Besides, her parents were very strict, so we never really had the opportunity and resigned to just take advantage of whatever opportunity was present to press our lips together.

We were in love and we were teenagers! I had heard enough songs to know that was what teenagers did or were supposed to do. I still believed we were good kids.

The night of the escapade on ice, never thinking we would reach a point where it would affect anything, I had painted a few stripes of the deodorant I had been wearing across my chest. In my mind, the scent of "musk" was very adult and alluring. I ignored the logic that maybe musk in cologne or aftershave form was adult and alluring, but it was probably not meant to be delicately slathered across the torso.

"My tongue feels really dry!" Barbara was frantically indicating past her outstretched tongue. I had forgotten about the deodorant and hadn't foreseen the current circumstances.

"Whuth's ongh yull cheth?" she slurred.

"Oh, right," I replied.

L (part 2)

I was being viciously admonished by my wife (which I had and did have for the previous seven and a half years) in my study (which I had, and did have for the past three years), in my house, in a town in Maine, where I lived with my wife. This was not a life I imagined. I have an active imagination, but the anger driving her words at me now in the venue chosen for it was beyond comprehension to me.

We need to back up. Follow me, please, to the origin of the path that led to where I now stood.

"My roommate has a crush on you."

I did not know her and figured by the communicative property I did not know her roommate, either. I had dog-eared her as a girl I would talk to if I were trying to talk to girls that night, except I wasn't. I was moving to where colloquialisms rained down and the heat is a damp heat. Plus, her roommate was not currently present, and whoever this person talking to me was present (and stunning), so I was willing to entertain further questioning and admissions.

She was striking: tattoos scampering up and down her arms, rings appearing and disappearing from her earlobes and nose, silver hair. She had silver hair! I should take this opportunity to explain although she was older than me, something revealed to me as the conversation we were now having developed into something more than names and neighborhoods where we lived, her hair was not naturally silver. She was a welcome visual oasis in this dark and dingy venue.

This place was paramount in the incubation of my tenure as a "greaser." Here, I hustled an unfortunate rube at pinball; had countless underage gins and tonics in plastic cups been adopted as a disciple by a few of the female regulars; warned about another female regular they called "Hatchet Face;" saw a wealth of the kinds of bands that rolled up my sleeves, cuffed my jeans, and filled my hair with the thickest of grease. I loved this place and all it represented.

In addition to authentic, suffocating grime, it presented the silver-haired angel before me now. Had it not been for the watery cocktails that graciously embraced the citrus nectar that still coated my finger and thumb, I would have been too nervous to do anything but imagine what might be. But gin and tonic coursed through my veins, and I was (disingenuously) comfortable.

She had just graduated from the art school downtown and was now planning to travel to assorted record labels dotted across the country in search of employment.

"Well, I'm moving to Carrboro, North Carolina on Friday, and Mammoth Records' world headquarters is there. If you visit them, and are in Carrboro, here's my phone number and my address."

To be continued...

XXIII

She was the only girlfriend I ever had my mom didn't like.

Correction: she was never my girlfriend and my mother didn't outright say she didn't like her, but she didn't outwardly endorse our relationship, either. That was a big deal. My mom liked every girlfriend I ever had. I didn't have many, but she supported my decisions, no matter how bad they were. I don't know why I was ever nervous introducing any romantic interest to her; she always welcomed them with open arms, usually literally. She'd call them "daughter" in the same initial conversation as meeting them. Not Angela. My mother's a smart woman. She knew. Maybe not specifics, but she knew enough. Because she couldn't, or wouldn't, say anything bad about anyone, she said Angela was "Rubenesque." My mom isn't the thinnest woman, either, but she meant it as a compliment. It was the nicest thing she came up with. No, she didn't say it to her. They didn't talk much. Or maybe they did, and something came out, maybe under questioning and mom judged her for it. Maybe she told my mom she was going to take my V Card. Probably not, but she was insightful. Anyway, no, my mom is insightful, not Angela. Angela sucks and she is evil.

Yeah, once and it was good, but we're getting off track here. Focus!

My mom being insightful made being sneaky tough; probably why I was such a good kid.

Angela sucks. For example, she had a boyfriend the whole time! We would be out in public in the middle of the day holding hands! She would kiss me on busy streets! I don't know if he knew.

Probably not. I didn't know. She was a liar. With everything she was, she told falsehoods. Yeah, I know.

I helped her dye her hair, too. Vampire's Blood. How prophetic. No, pr 'fedik. I don't think it was the same night, but she had me over to watch a movie. Valley Girl. She was surprised I didn't try to have sex with her. She was very vocal about it. She said, "Most guys would have had my clothes off by now." Just not me. I don't know. I essentially had a breakdown in front of her. I was upset because we were so different. I felt like I just kept saying, "But you're bad and I'm good." I don't know what it meant. I didn't even know how right I was.

Yeah, she put her mouth on me. It was only the second time anyone ever had. No, I didn't. I'm sure she was disappointed, but who cares? Imagine what was probably down there! It probably had fangs! I don't know. She was totally naked, and I wasn't going to do anything like what she wanted. I know, but you know that. Besides, it would've been my first time. I'm sure I would've been terrible at it.

I only found it out later; she made it her mission to get my V Card. Shut up, you know what I'm talking about. My V Card. Figure it out. V Card. You know what it means. Think back to... well, probably never, but somebody used to say it. Well, I did! I do, I guess. Well, once she figured out that she wasn't going to get it, she tried to pawn me off on one of her roommates. No, Mandy. No, she is, but what an asshole! No, I mean Angela is an asshole. Mandy's sweet. But who does that?!? There was something else, too, but there didn't need to be. I had pretty much figured out at that point, with time and reflection (and Mom's motherly insight), that she was no good. Holding hands and kissing in broad daylight! What an asshole.

I have. I went to that high-priced bullshitty, trendy clothing place. Yeah, that one. She worked there, and I was trying on shoes. She was helping. She had just gotten her cheek pierced. It was all red and swollen still. I said to her, "Oh, look. I think the turkey's done!" Yeah, he loved it. He was a little embarrassed, kept wondering why I was being so mean to her. Yeah, she brought out these big clunky shoes for me to try on and I asked if they came with bolts for my neck, too. Yeah, Frankenstein. We left and I didn't buy anything anyway. I know, all their stuff's too trendy and whatever. We went to the Doc Marten store. Yeah, it was great. No, they were great shoes. Yeah, those. I know! He kept wanting to fuck around and it was a birthday party! In the dorms! They got all scuffed up! Yeah, I pinned him down and choked him a little, but still! No, but they're great shoes. They say "SATAN RESISTENT" on the bottom. I know, she probably would've started smoking and shaking like the guy at the end of Indiana Jones. I know. She sucked.

XXIV, XXV, & XXVI

It was my birthday again. I had one every year.

I didn't have a party every year, but Kara insisted that she throw one for me and that I attend. I put her in charge of the guest list and the music. I stated that it was my birthday and thus I had veto power over the music. When one of my favorite tunes came on (a classic), she became visibly distraught and exercised her veto power, which she did not have. Upon questioning and voiced disapproval, she provided no details but made it very clear that her reaction was spurred by a traumatic event.

What a shame, I thought. *Such a great song.*

I brought a shiny, metallic blue, blank journal and some crayons so everyone in attendance could leave birthday wishes. My friends were creative people and when embellished and warped by alcohol, I knew the results would be, at the very least, entertaining.

I didn't look at the book until the next day, and when I did, it revealed plans and outlined things that were way too adult to be written in crayon. The most mature of which came from a girl who was partnered with a guy who delivered pharmaceuticals to old folks' homes. He was, himself, a card-carrying member of a methadone clinic and probably not someone who should have access to the medication of the elderly.

I knew them from the coffee shop where I worked with Kara and several of the other partygoers. The girl's entry in my birthday book had an ethereal, ghostlike female (nude) and notification that "she had my periwinkle crayon and if I wanted it back..."

Just like that. It didn't say anything else and I reasoned that it didn't really need to. I'm not always the quickest to pick up on such things, sometimes intentionally so, but the message was clear, and I took no steps to retrieve the crayon.

Another was from Sophie and was prognostically narrating the actions of Kara. The girls and their other roommate, Minnie, were the documented residents of the domicile. I didn't know Minnie terribly well and if she didn't live in the house where the party was held, she probably would not have been invited. Well, she might have been invited by someone else or have been dating someone I knew or was loosely friends with. She was cute, though self-preservation kept her predominantly reserved and not open to flirtations.

I know this personally because I was in the kitchen with her on another night after another party. She was applying lip balm and I asked if I could use some. She extended her arm with the small cylinder in hand and I said, "No, I'd rather have it from the tap." Then we kissed...briefly. Upon retrospection, I could not believe the line led to anything other than an eye roll. Maybe pepper spray, but kisses? No.

That night led to one third of the residents of 143 Awl Street being kissed. Tonight, was my birthday party and although I blew out candles and made a wish, it was not that the other two fall into the same category of "kissed."

Had I read the birthday book the actual day of my birthday, I could have prepared. I would have known about Sophie and Kara's plans and mentally conjured up polite escapes. I would have had time to think things over and make according plans, but no, I just marinated in a few more birthday drinks and the self-satisfaction of the birthday book's existence.

Sophie sat down next to me on the couch, wearing a smile that could have meant any number of things, none of which were admitted to by churchgoers. She was a cute girl, a little heavier than I would have preferred (especially sober), but she had a big, eager smile. It was genuine. and I liked to both see it and be the reason for it.

She was perpetually single and always eager to tell that to anyone. She had planned, made amendments to, and re-planned the same imaginary wedding since she was a child. Her desperation was hindering it from ever actually happening.

She sat next to me and grinned. You could almost hear a voice in her head repeating, "It's happening! Stay calm. Breathe. It's really happening!" She stopped grinning long enough for us to kiss. It was nice.

Sophie and I had kissed before, one very surreal afternoon when we went into a heavily drug-themed movie under the bright sunlight and came out to a torrential downpour. The theatre was on the deep incline (or decline, depending on your point of view) of a large hill that stretched several blocks.

The raging river barreling down the slanted street mandated the removal of shoes, socks, and eventually, wet clothing. It would have been chivalrous, but it was her car, so she took off her shoes and socks first and braved the rapids to retrieve it, assuming it had not washed away.

Surprisingly, it had not washed away, and she pulled up near the sidewalk, leaving enough room for me to soak my now bare leg about halfway to my knee as I braved the short trip to the passenger's seat. She leaned over, unlocked my door, and pushed it open just far enough to leave it vulnerable to the breakers.

The seat had quickly made the transition from damp to drenched under the unexpected storm and through the opened windows. It was a moot point since both of us were already soaked to the skin and sweating under our old jeans and thrift store button-up shirts.

When we returned to my apartment, I lent her a dry t-shirt shirt, a pair of jeans that inexperience and a lack of preparedness had seen shredded by a bicycle chain, and a leather belt from an Army surplus store. Before she dressed in dry clothes, my dry clothes, we kissed for long enough to let the wrinkles dry in our skin and clothes.

My birthday was weeks later, and I still had not gotten my belt back. I liked that belt and it complemented the weathered old steel-toed work shoes I had inherited from my father. They were beat to hell and I took every advantage I could to add further signs of manual labor to them. I didn't have a job in a factory or anything, but I was a barback and would routinely kick kegs in order to further mar the shoes.

Sophie came into the darkened living room and sat down on the couch, on my left side. The party had run its course and I certainly didn't realize it at the time, but the mass exodus might have been initiated by Sophie and Kara. It was their place and unlike the censorship of songs, controlling lingering party guests and overall crowd flow was certainly within their realm.

Kara took a close seat on my right side and began to busy herself with an unnecessary intricate task of some sort as Sophie and I kissed. It wasn't much, and Kara seemed to be quietly approving of the situation.

I could almost hear her smiling and anticipating as well, so I turned my head. I played it off like it was no big whoop, no big thing, but I was kissing, turning, kissing, turning, back and forth between two girls! They weren't right next to each other, but we were all on the same couch and it was a small couch! I was amused by it when thinking back and recounting the story. I called the couch a loveseat. Wink.

I was less amused by the existence of Jonah, Kara's boyfriend. He and I weren't friends, and I found him rather abrasive and condescending, but it didn't give me the right to fool around with his girlfriend and her roommate/best friend and denigrate their relationship.

Kara, Sophie, and I then kissed (and more) on a few other occasions and it was accepted and agreed upon that it was our secret. No one else needed to know. No one else should know—not my friends, not their friends, and certainly not Jonah.

The first time it happened...wait, that makes it seem like an accident. The first time we messed around and had planned it, I thought the novelty of it was appealing. After that, I felt bad because of Jonah and because of the reputation the events would spawn if anyone knew. Things were said about people who partook in such things. Had I not been one of the involved parties, I would have made judgement-fueled jokes and snide comments. I could see it now, with raised eyebrows and a gaping mouth, I would have acted shocked and maybe a bit repulsed. But, because it was me, I was a mélange of thumbs-ups of coolness and a lowered head of shame and regret.

To some people it isn't a big deal, but those people are usually in movies I don't watch, and they went much farther than we ever did. To us, and I can only speak definitively for myself, it's too big of a deal to keep silent. I did, however, but they couldn't, and didn't withhold for very long.

Word got out and around and back to me from someone who was agreeing and applauding the whole affair. I sternly denied his requests for tutelage and went to speak with the girls.

They knew I was upset and understood why without me ever having to say anything directly to them. That further supported my logic for insisting we keep it to ourselves. Sophie, Kara, and Jonah came into the restaurant where I worked and had previously lived above, and I walked in as they were leaving. Jonah was well within his right to punch me, maybe repeatedly, in the face, when I passed him. Thankfully, he did not.

I didn't look at or speak to the girls and I didn't want to play too near Jonah in the tiger's cage by saying more than three words. I owed him so much more of an apology and statement of regret, but I just looked at him and said, "I'm sorry, man."

L (part 3)

My mother had accompanied me in the moving truck to chaperone me and all my worldly possessions to my new home down south. She was always eager to help, and bursting with encouragement, even for decisions that were questionable at best. I'm certain she would have contrived a way to transport my things even if I had not been present to do so, so I suppose I was accompanying her.

I repaid her generosity by endlessly droning on about "this girl I met a few nights ago! She had silver hair and was beautiful!" I appreciate the relationship I have with my Mother (as well as her limitless parental charity), and her patience as she listened to the menagerie of "this girl I met" and "she had purple hair!" and potential I clearly believed was present, but was usually only present in my imagination.

Though she had all my necessary contact information, I never realistically expected to hear from the mysterious vixen from the bar.

The next two weeks found me securing a hospitality position at a prominent restaurant and microbrewery in the heart of the historic university town next to my new neighborhood. It was walking distance, but I quickly learned it was a distance which would mandate a brief reprieve in the walk-in cooler when I finally arrived at work. I had been introduced to the effects of a blazing sun on all sorts of petroleum-based hair-coiffing substances when I picked up the application, and became a sweaty, oily expert when I walked it back. I was hired anyway, but I felt gross.

I developed a steady routine of joining a co-worker for bil-liards and drinking, and there was not always a co-worker, and not always billiards. I enjoyed companionship, and I had always enjoyed billiards, but I think I might have liked drinking a bit too much a bit too often. I was aware it was only two weeks but commencing a new life with bad habits is not a good idea.

The night I vomited down the length of my burly fabric cur-tains from my loft bed, and awoke with a macaroni noodle in my nostril, I decided I would decelerate my relationship with alcohol. I reconsidered my newfound camaraderie with my functional alcoholic billiard partner as well.

To be continued...

XXVII

It was the Christmas party at work. "Work" was a coffee shop and it was pretty tame, so it wasn't like an office party where that guy from accounting got drunk and showed everyone his balls or Irene from Accounts Receivable had too many daiquiris (like one and a half) and took off her top. There was alcohol there, but the people who made a routine of calling in hungover were behaving.

Cassie was a cutie. She had curly light brown hair down past her shoulders and an excited, but vapid, look on her face...always.

"Psst. Hey, Cassie! Come here!"

I was standing on the stairs, peeking around the corner where the French presses and stupid little travel mugs were on display. The managers' office, the bathrooms, and a handful of the tables that overlooked the counter and people ordering and receiving drinks and pastries were the only things upstairs. There was a short hallway that led past the bathrooms to the office. It was the only thing I was interested in upstairs, at least until Cassie came up.

She was smiling but looked confused. She always looked like someone had said something funny she didn't get but laughed at anyway. She was not laughing to be polite or false, she was just laughing at something else that she got, but no one else did.

"Yeah, Cassie."

"Yeah, great, but she's dumb."

My co-worker was injecting his unwanted opinion on the happenings and on the subject of it.

"No, she's not. She's cute."

"Don't you remember when she put whole beans in the basket and put it in the coffee machine? Didn't weigh it, didn't grind it. She's dumb."

"That wasn't her. That was the blonde girl, the dumb one."

I was relieved and eager to clear her reputation.

"What?"

"That wasn't her. That was the other girl, the…the blonde one. I don't remember her name. I worked at the other store when she worked here. I never worked with her. I know she was dumb, though. Cute, but dumb. She did it. I remember hearing about it."

"Well, Cassie's not a brain surgeon."

"I'm not saying she is, but she's cute and I think she's smarter than she lets on."

"She'd have to be. Wait, why does that matter if she's cute? She can be cute and dumb. A lot of girls are. And Hannah was her name."

"I never worked with her. You're right, but she's got something there, like something behind those eyes."

"Sure. You're hopeless. You're a moron and so is she."

"We kissed at the Christmas party."

He shook his head, knowing defeat.

XXVIII

He didn't even know what day it was when the doctor questioned him, and the doctor had to ask multiple times to divert his attention from the lined wallpaper he was staring at. He looked up at the doctor, asked "What?" again, and answered with an optimistic guess that was days away from correct.

He hadn't been able to swallow on his own for the past day and night. To aid in the grueling task of forcing saliva down his own throat, he sought the help of a crowd of oversized plastic tumblers full of sports drink. He would sip out of them and the added liquid would make his throat work again, like the flushing of a toilet. This was the third time he had seen a doctor and the third doctor he had seen. At present, he couldn't remember ever seeing the other two and wouldn't remember this one as soon his attention went back to the thin, parallel lines that ran up the wall.

The doctor asked him something else, but he was fixed on the symmetry of the pattern and his mother answered for him. She did so quickly, as if shortening the time between words would result in a more rapid resolution.

The doctor withdrew his attention from the young man and addressed the mother directly. "He should go to the hospital for some blood work and a few tests. I'm going to have Tracey call over and let them know you're coming." The car ride was through a similar mental fog. Trees and houses and signs and eateries and other cars ran by the window and he just watched the blur of them. His mother spoke to him through the fog, but her words slowed as they struggled through until they were slurs and incoherencies by the time they reached him. He just sat gazing blankly though the window as his mouth filled with saliva.

In the examining room, his temperature, blood pressure, height, and weight were recorded, and he was left to wait. His mother requested, at his muddled prompting, a glass of water from the nurse. He still could not swallow on his own and had, over the course of the silent car ride, lost the ability to adequately form the sounds that comprise coherent speech. His loose, sloppy words frightened his mother and she labored over whether to leave him to find a nurse and discuss the urgency of this development in private. She could have screamed it while sitting next to him and he would not have reacted, but she opted to leave and spare him her disquieting alarm.

She returned to comfort him with news he would not understand and promises he could not appreciate. He was raising his hand high in the air and focusing his gaze on it, then watching it slowly fall back down to his stomach. He raggedly explained that it was the only way he could control where his eyes looked. When his hand met his stomach and his vision left it, his eyes would float back up into his head. His mother hurried, crying, out of the room and he was ushered with great haste upstairs to a room and a bed that moved up and down.

After a brief examination by a doctor whose plans that evening were not scheduled to include looking down the nose and, upon failing, the throat of the young man, he turned to answer the desperate mother.

"Do you think he got it from kissing his girlfriend? Her name's Brie. I know she's had this once before."

"If she had it once before, chances are it immunized her and she's well past the contagious stage. I doubt she had it this bad," answered the doctor, who had diverted his attention to the now-soiled instruments he was cleaning and putting away.

The doctor interrupted the mother's follow-up question to push a button. Instantly, the bed was being rolled quickly to a destination the boy was not aware of. He was surrounded by bodies in white coats and soft blue V-necks and they were rushing him and his bed down a hallway. Some were speaking to each other hastily, some were speaking to his parents hastily, and one was speaking to him, slowly, and showing him a long plastic tube. "We're going to insert this tube into your throat, so you can breathe, okay?"

Hindered by astonishment, bewilderment, and the failure of his mechanisms, he gathered what he could to ask, "Are you going to cut me?"

"No. We aren't going to cut you."

Before beginning to count backwards from 100, as instructed, he thought of the tube and its relation, in size, to his neck. As he inhaled and sputtered inside the thick mask, he wondered, How are they going to get that in me without cutting me?

———

His mental lack of acceptance of the size discrepancy between his throat and the tube was echoed by his body, which, without cognizant thought, coughed and gagged the tube out of his esophagus. This happened repeatedly, and a chemical was introduced into him that rendered his body a tranquil, completely immobile vessel for the tube and chemicals that surged through him. He was now rendered unconscious—as he had been for nearly a day—and paralyzed, but he was not gagging, nor was he aware of any of this.

———

Family encircled him, intermittently interrupted by the occasional white-coated body holding a clipboard. Tubes scurried out

Nicholas J. Stevens

of him and snaked into him. Lights blinked. Machines bleeped. He was a serene mound of young man gently rising and falling underneath the knit blanket. Then, he woke up.

He woke up and saw only black. He was awake but cloaked in impossibly dark confusion. He thought he was awake. He could feel his insides working—his heart pumping, his lungs taking in air, his blood moving through him, or maybe he didn't. He had never really focused on the state of being alive and, thus, he wasn't sure that he was alive. He had never been dead before and didn't know what you felt or didn't feel, but this was certainly nothing like the accounts of being dead he had ever heard. He couldn't open his eyes. He couldn't sit up. He couldn't wave to anyone who could help him or at least explain to him that he was dead. He couldn't move. He saw only black.

It was nothing like a dream. In dreams, you could see images, hear sounds, fly, fall, scream, laugh, and interact as if you were living. He saw only black. He couldn't fly, wasn't falling, and couldn't scream. He tried.

He had to go to the bathroom! Maybe this was proof he was alive! This yearning served as his only assurance that he was alive. But he was conditioned for years, so much so that it became an actual learned instinct, to stand in front or something, usually attached to plumbing, to expel himself. He didn't want to make a mess. He didn't want to be confined to a pool of his own waste, unable to move.

He tried desperately to motion to someone or something to aid him. He concentrated and funneled his efforts into desperately fulfilling his social habituation. He was unaware that another tube had eradicated his need for concern. He did not know it was expected and, therefore, prevented. He did not know he needn't fight his motionless body or scream in frustration at the smothering black. He didn't know why he couldn't move. Through the closed slits of his gray, tranquil face, he flowed. Past his quiet cheeks and matted hair, the pillow began to dampen.

"Oh my God! He's up!"

XXIX

He is cute.

He has kind of a Grease retro thing happening and I can't tell if it's a character or if it really is him. I know tons of those kinds of girls and it takes a lot of work to look the way they do. Thing is, it's a lot of primping and curling and uncomfortably squeezing into old clothes, or clothes that are supposed to look old, but fall apart when you do. It's cute, I guess. That is, if they succeed in achieving the look they're going for.

I could do it, I just don't want to. Well, not all the time.

I'll play the part, too, and I'm going to have him over and be all vintage-y and ridiculous together. I'll start us off with some drinks from that bartending book I got at the library book sale, then see what happens. I've never really made any of them and I can only drink maybe two of them, but I'm not planning on just drinking all night. What fun is that unless I'm out with the girls?

I've seen those fancy drinks made in movies all the time and it doesn't look too hard. I can use that little lunch box thermos I have to shake up the drinks and maybe I'll stop and get some of those little plastic mermaids to put on the sides of the glasses. They have monkeys, too, and I should decide what I'm going to make so I can choose the appropriate ornament. I'll get both and he can choose. I'll bet he chooses the monkey. What a primate! Maybe I'll dress like Betty Rubble, but sexy. No, that's whorish.

I hope I'm not giving him the wrong idea by asking him to come over, getting him drunk, getting all twirled up, and playing records for him. Whether or not I'm oozing the wrong vibe depends entirely on the records. I have some in mind. Okay, honestly, I know for a fact which records I'll play, and which one will be the perfect one that will make him want to take our shirts off and rub against each other.

But I don't want to be just another girl. I'm special and he better know that!

I know he gets around. I'll bet. I mean, I don't know it for a fact and I don't personally know anyone that has...done things with him...or for him...or to him. I don't have any proof or anything, but he's so cute in his apron, combing his hair in the mirror next to the espresso machine. I'll bet he puts more time (and grease) in his hair than any guy or girl I know, not that I know a lot of either who put grease in their hair. But he's a little pretty boy. He's delicious.

I really have to actually ask him over.

What if he has plans with some other little tart tonight? This is a kind of a spur-of-the-moment operation, but I'm sure he'll choose me anyway. He'll swagger through my door in his rolled-up jeans with his rolled-up sleeves and leather shoes. I'll make us cocktails, he'll be impressed by my bartending prowess, and he will want to put his mouth on my mouth.

I guess it would mean he has to go home and change first. I'm fine if he just comes over smelling like coffee and man smell and pomade. I like coffee and I like the smell of pomade, even the thick kind not made from anything "natural." I remember asking him once and him being way too into talking about it and rambling on and on about it. I wonder if I run my hands through his hair if he'll bite me. Hmm, maybe.

"Hi! Do you want to come over later? I got some new records and a Star Wars lunch box with a thermos. I can make us drinks."

"Yeah, tonight? Sure, that sound great. Where do you live and when?"

"I live in Squirrel Hill...all the time?"

He looks confused. But, wow, I can't believe he actually agreed to that! Not my best work, but...

I'll write it down for him on a napkin like in the movies. I would kiss it and leave an imprint of lipstick, but I'm not wearing any. Maybe I'll put some on so when I kiss him, he'll know it! It'll be a bright red reminder every time he looks in the mirror. I mean, until he washes his face. What am I saying, he doesn't wash his face.

That's three cocktails! Like in martini cocktails! He seems fine. He is fine.

That picture looks crooked. I'll just lean over and...

"Oh, hello!"

"Hi. Going to straighten your picture?"

"It can wait. Set your drink down for a second."

Go for it, Amanda! Just do it!

"Here."

Amanda mouth meet Greasy Boy mouth.

Um, he tastes like vodka. I taste, like, mandarin oranges in his mouth, like those kind from a can, but I didn't use any mandarin oranges. I don't think I did. I don't think I own any. I don't think I've ever...

Whoa! Somebody's givin' me the world tour—Russian (rushin') hands and Roman (roamin') fingers! That's interest—

Um, no... Cool your jets, slick.

"That kind of hurts."

L (part 4)

Half of a single month (two weeks) passed by with, predictably, no correspondence from the divine being the heavens sent to me only two days before leaving. I repeated her name as I told and retold the endearing, but uneventful story of our meeting in an unsuccessful attempt to summon her. "Violet this" and "Violet that," and "Violet did that thing" or "Violet was doing this thing" in a futile attempt to somehow produce her. The myth about repeating a name and the being showing up was exclusively reserved for demons, but that aspect of the myth escaped me, so I kept trying. Plus, she had made quite an impression on me, and I had employed desperate measures to see her again.

Then, she called. She called me, and we talked. We talked for hours, and we told stories everyone we even sparsely knew had long since grown tired of. We told jokes that had become even less funny with the thinness of repetition. We talked and made plans to talk more.

A welcome bout of incidental sobriety emerged because I stayed home to talk to her on the telephone and declined invitations to shoot billiards and drink alcohol. Again, billiards was merely an ancillary activity participated in between beverages. I would stagger up to the table, lean over it, straighten back up, refocus on a nonexistent object on an opposing wall all while doing my very best Paul Newman impression (which looked absolutely nothing like him, and I'd have not sounded like him, either, because my impression was of a silent, stoic Paul Newman), and my billiards prowess was novice. But, she called, and listened to my stories and jokes.

We shared aspirations, and hers included visiting the record label in the town where I lived. This meant she would be coming to the town where I lived. I would offer her a place to stay because I had ample space for a guest and I was a cordial host. The thought occurred to me she would be driving a business days' worth of driving, and if she did stay overnight, and did so in my humble abode, we could or perhaps even would cuddle. If we cuddled, it might, perhaps, potentially, hypothetically, lead to kissing. Why stop at first base? It seemed natural for mouths to open and hands to mosey, then we were making out. This was as far as I took reality-based fantasies, but I could realistically believe in an inevitability of us making out.

This was all contingent upon her deciding to drive several hundred miles, and me not saying anything stupid enough before she did to make her not want to.

To be continued...

XXX

It was her cousin I had a crush on; a crush that perpetually regenerated for seven days every year.

The adults took off 10 days from their respective jobs, but we drove there and back, so the in-person crush portion of vacation was only a week. I didn't see her the other 358 days of the year and we didn't keep in touch, so I anticipated it before it happened and missed it when it was over. There wasn't really an "it" to look forward to or miss, but I greatly anticipated the potential my imagination created before I saw her and mourned its absence when it was gone. I teared up one previous year when "Surfer Girl" came on the radio and we had started our trip back to Ohio with the salt still in our noses. It was the same year I burned my shoulders and half my face because I didn't want to shift my attention away or stop looking at her or whatever part of her, she intentionally exposed to the glaring sun. I like her and burned me.

She didn't attend "the beach" (as the family called it) this year, but neither did my cousin, the match my family had consecrated for Daisy. Their non-attendance produced a coupling bred of convenience, though neither Daisy nor I objected. Instead, she invited a friend to join my other cousin and I on an excursion to play mini-golf.

It was obvious to anyone besides Daisy or me that my cousin was not as excited about his pairing or role as accompaniment to us. The friend was desperately excited about the prospect, however, and the imbalance had rapidly become a drain on the fun my cousin should have been having.

Nicholas J. Stevens

It was a stunning day and if I had not been so preoccupied with Daisy and she had not been so preoccupied with her friend's amusement, I would have noticed or cared. I would have effortlessly declared it a perfect day for outdoor activities, but nice days on vacation were subconsciously just expected.

It was either my disregard for the opinions or authority of the high school kids that ran the mini-golf course, my own desire for public attention, or my longing to impress a family member, but I stretched my putter up and around my neck until it was perpendicular to the ground. The small, fluorescent pink golf ball that lay at my feet seemed just as confused as my teammates until I pulled the club around in a large, circular motion and sent it with a click into the adjoining yard.

"Oh, golly, I'm hot today!"

A delightful blend of sincere enjoyment, terror, and confusion washed over their faces. If I had been looking at anything other than where my ball ended up and whether it had broken anything on its journey, I would have noticed them searching for the questions they wanted to ask. I had no legitimate, reasonable answers to offer anyway, so it worked out.

The glowing ember of sunlight over, then past, us had been replaced by the glowing pearl of moonlight smiling at us now. My interest in Daisy had been changing and growing over the few days of this current vacation and she became more than an ensemble member with every stretch, smile, and bend to pick up golf balls. Her potential now shone, and she was in the spotlight.

She and I agreed to find a vacant set of stairs under the moonlight and "set a spell," as they say in her parts...I think. My cousin and her friend followed our unspoken instructions and walked farther down the sand to their own vacant deck.

Finally, Daisy and I were completely alone in arguably (and unintentionally) the most romantic setting imaginable. We were sitting on wooden stairs only feet from the sand and only yards from a sporadically waving ocean. It truthfully didn't have to be as idyllic as it was—we were two attractive teenagers whose attraction had been growing for years.

It didn't take long for me to lean in and grab hold of the bulb of her lips in between mine. This led to my hands sliding the length of her sides and the silken fabric that covered it.

She was wearing jeans and my costume this year included a chain of rolled up strips of magazine and a pair of daisy-covered boxer shorts I wore over a pair of briefs. I had other clothes with me, too, on other days, but most of my vacation saw me dressed only in a swimsuit.

I was glad it was night and that our plans didn't involve standing because my daisy-covered boxers were now occasionally graced by the real Daisy and my reaction would have been more than a little embarrassing. The real Daisy didn't seem to mind, and she ran her hands over the bouquet I was wearing as pants while making sounds in between the aural crashing of waves. If there was a female equivalent to what I was wearing or how my body reacted to her, she was the one who would have been red-faced with embarrassment. Luckily, there exists no such thing and it was a clandestine endeavor.

There was stiffness in the flower garden and it took everything, everything, to maintain my internal and external composure. Daisy's bold and intentional hand tightened quickly, then released slowly a scant few times until I cringed, then released... once...a second, dampening time...and a few more times as my face bent what was supposed to be a smile into something wrenched and ridiculous.

I apologized as my hand went toward the stiff crease of her jeans. It moved up a few inches as I pulled at the flap of denim holding the metal button in place. She made an intoxicated, exhausted sound as she strained to fight what she hoped would continue.

"I'm on my..." She stopped there.

Nicholas J. Stevens

She didn't have to say anything else. I understood, and with the same hand, and now the necessary assistance of the other, I re-buttoned her jeans. I slowly slid my hand back down her thigh towards her knee, pausing to feel the warmth where the creases of her jeans met.

With disappointment on her windy voice, she sighed, "You're drivin' me crazy."

I would have to wait until next year.

XXXI

We were all good kids and since our parents knew we weren't going to do anything harmful to ourselves or anyone else, they signed off on our unapproved absence from school. They even carpooled to pick us up!

Gertie had an in-ground pool, so the decision to spend our day of truancy at her house was an easy one to make. It was close to the last summer we had together before we scattered, went off to various colleges and universities in various places, and lost contact with members of the group we didn't see or must see or really want to see daily. Some of those present got a little teary-eyed when the topic of immediate and extended futures was brought up. I did not.

The party, if it was one, was strategically planned to satisfy all the stereotypical trappings of a pool party. There were crinkling plastic bags of various chips emptied into large wooden bowls or left in their bags, maladroitly prepared (and possibly hazardous) items from the unsupervised grill, assorted pool toys, non-alcoholic beverages (because we were all good kids), and a variety of cards and party games. It was as if someone had read an instruction manual on how to throw a pool party for ethical youths and followed it strictly...which someone in our group probably did.

Only one or two of those in attendance were ever invited or had ever attended parties thrown by kids outside our social group from the other side of the tracks. Those parties had beer and the grills would have been the only things supervised, though the food, if there was any, came in boxes delivered by other kids who were also not invited. Since we had no frame of reference and our only comparisons to such parties came predominantly from popular movies and television, we were unaware how unsophisticated and boringly uneventful our party was. I mean, we were skipping school, so wasn't that an event?!

Time spent in the pool was only scandalous in the mind of the adolescent males in attendance and would only be explored in quiet places well away from the party. During the party, the boys were gentlemen who might occasionally look, but would never stare, at suits that slipped or areas of bodies that were covered during school hours.

After we had tired and our hunger for snacks and inherently uncooked ground meat grew, we adjourned to the well-lit, ornately decorated house. There were paper plates and napkins set out next to the embroidered napkins that had no utility whatsoever. The condiments were there, too. Anticipating many more attendees than were there, several sleeves of plastic cups of varying sizes and colors were also present. I made the grievous error of using a glass made of glass and was disciplined by the hosts' glares.

We ate, laughed, and chose to stay indoors to engage in what we considered "more adult" entertainment. The game in question involved going into an unlit closet with someone of the opposite sex and doing...something. The rules were replaced by giggles, so I wasn't 100 percent certain. I did have thoughts, though.

My accomplice for this randomly-selected ribaldry was Gertie, my friend and the host of this poolside soiree. We were often in the same places, watching the same shows, listening to the same music, and having the same snacks, but we never really spent time alone, just the two of us. There was certainly never any latent physical chemistry to explain away or discuss.

She did slap me in the face once freshman year, but upon re-examining the series of events with a different mind, I totally deserved it.

The door closed and again her hands were on the sides of my face, but this time it was to guide my smiling and nervous mouth into her eager and self-satisfied one. No words were spoken and there was pulling and rubbing, but no clothing was removed. I mean, we only had the limited, pre-ordained amount of time and didn't want to be partially clothed when an abruptly opened door exposed us. We would have justifiably been accused of taking this PG-13 party to a full PG.

Her boyfriend, who resembled a popular late-night talk show host (but much bigger) was in attendance and seemed to tolerate whatever went on in the closet. He publicly asked no questions, but probably posed more probing inquiries to Gertie in private. Even privately, though, he didn't ask me any questions.

He knew just as well as the rest of the coterie of nerds that what went on in the closet required no explanation to him or anyone else.

Nicholas J. Stevens

XXXII

In a darkened dorm room, we sat in a tight circle and listened to Connie explain why it was about to get much darker. She distributed handfuls of uncooked beans and explained the rules, if you could call them that, of Innocence.

Connie was adorable. No wait, Connie was adorable. She always wore a smile like she had just gotten away with something. She was ornery. She wasn't beautiful, like tall and slender with a shine of long, silken hair cascading over her exceptionally perfect posture. She wasn't traditionally beautiful and, in fact, was quite the opposite. She was short, she had perpetual bed head, and she had tiny sneakers on her tiny feet. She was adorable, like a teddy bear, and she was perfect to a cuddle with.

She stayed over once when I lived with Sascha, the model (who was that kind of beautiful) and we cuddled and kissed. Me and Connie, not me and Sascha! She was out of my league. I was pretty sure Connie and I weren't going to be sleepover friends or kiss again, but I wanted to be special to her. I wanted her to talk about me and tell stories I was in.

This could be one of those stories. The lights were to be extinguished entirely and we were to all sit less than an arm's distance away from a rigid ceramic bowl. We were then supposed to drop the uncooked beans into the bowl when we had done or experienced whatever the person speaking questioned.

The mood of the game swung wildly from jovial and playful to raw and uncomfortably personal. The instructions to "drop a bean" were quickly abandoned after the first few challenges were made.

Drop a bean if you've ever been peed on. There was a clink followed by "Ew!" and laughter. You were never supposed to identify or guess who dropped the bean, and that was the reason the game was played entirely in the dark. It was funny (sometimes), and accusations and challenges were made aloud (sometimes), but when the mood shifted, it was as silent as it was dark.

Have you ever been raped? At least two beans fell, and the honesty hit the bowl like gunfire. The results could be expected by more than a few of the attendees, and simple deduction would reveal the person who said it dropped one of the beans. I wanted to approach and comfort the speaker, but it was taboo to investigate their identity. It could also be reasonably assumed by the vehicle they chose to reveal it, they didn't want their identity unearthed, at least not publicly and at least not now.

Have you ever done a rusty trombone? Connie interrupted the silence and tension by introducing a revolting term she had found on the internet. She proceeded to explain, in sickening detail, exactly what it was, how it was done, and what actions it would lead or follow. She was laughing uncontrollably and saying the names of those friends she was certain had "done a rusty trombone." She would throw a bean at the person whose name she called, and Erin kept track of how many beans Connie was throwing so she could replace them when the next person spoke.

Drop a bean if you've ever gotten a Cleveland steamer? No beans dropped, but again Connie laughed, threw beans, and declared the recipients of the thrown beans "gross!"

"Rusty trombone! Two dogs in a bathtub! Buckin' bronco! Kentucky Klondike bar! Cold lunch! Mystery meat" It had degenerated to the point where Connie was just yelling terms, some of which she had obviously just made up, and throwing fistfuls of beans around the room while screeching and laughing madly.

Have you ever tried to commit suicide? A muffled, hesitant question found its way through Connie's sputtering squeals and grasping breaths. After the question was posed, the darkness was silent, except for Connie's waning panting and the sobering scintillation of at least two beans. No instructions to drop beans were given, but it was instinctual at this point in the exercise, so none were necessary. No one had "gone out" and revealed their guilt, and the game somberly went on.

Drop a bean if you've gone to work drunk. Beans dropped like machine gun fire, there was laughing, and the mood was lightened.

Drop a bean if you've ever pooped yourself. A few beans dropped, at least I hope they were beans.

...as an adult! Someone asked if they could retrieve their bean, but they were denied.

L (part 5)

Violet told me she "had to get out of town" and was coming to visit the record company in town and, consequently, me. I wasn't sure how these two phenomena ranked in order of importance to her, but by my reasoning, it didn't matter, and we were totally going to make out.

I failed to further question why she "had to get of town." Was she in trouble with the law? Feeling claustrophobic? Was she running from a crazy, violent ex-boyfriend? Was she running from a crazy, violent ex-girlfriend? That last option was, admittedly, kind of hot, but none of it mattered to me. Why she "had to get out of town" was irrelevant because she was gorgeous, would probably (definitely?) be sleeping in my bed next to me, and probably (hopefully) be kissing my mouth with hers. Maybe her crazy ex-girlfriend would show up, and they would playfully, sexily fight like in late night movies on cable television. I didn't think that last part would happen, and only recently conceived of it during private relaxation time. I was a human man after all.

I already asked if she needed or wanted a place to sleep, and she already accepted my offer to do so. I extended the offer without the expected trepidation or nervousness that should accompany the posing of an offer to sleep over to a beautiful woman, but I was unexpectedly unshaken when I did. Examination may have suggested my cavalier nature was a result of "verbal muscle memory," a thing which does not exist, stemming from the careless candor I shared when I had a few drinks and spoke freely.

Whatever the origin, I considered the entirety of the conversation, and our preceding conversations, successful.

To be continued...

XXXIII

The question is not, "Why are you wearing a beret?" The question is, "Why are you not wearing a beret?" After all, I'm the one sacrificing a beautifully coiffed, shiny pompadour.

In my mind, artists wear berets...at the least the good ones. Alley was far more artistically apt than I was, but I wanted to make Christmas cards, too. Tully did, and I wanted to, too. His was just an enlarged black and white photo of his smiling face ringed by the words "MERRY CHRISTMAS HAPPY HANNUKAH BITCHIN' KWANZAA" repeated in a swirl to the edges of the card, but I wanted to make a Christmas card of my own.

I used to "draw" when I was younger, but it was mostly just "freehand tracing," not drawing, and not really art. I would look at an image, study it, then re-create it on a separate sheet of paper. At the time, I thought it was art, and fooled myself into believing I had artistic talent. Maybe it was talent, but only a talent at replicating, not creating. After seeing Alley's portfolio, it became more than obvious what I used to do was not art.

I did use to create and draw out stick figure wars that spanned feet of computer paper, the kind connected by un-ripped, perforated lines. The tiny, battling men were too small to have faces, but were adorned with tiny hats or helmets made by either bisecting their heads (helmets), or bisecting their heads with a line stretching slightly longer on one side (hats). The headgear was how you could tell what side they fought on and for.

Alley was from a different part of my depressing Midwest state, and I had only been to her town once. It was for a bowling tournament with an androgynous teammate (soccer and bowling) my mother thought was a girl and addressed him so. He was a boy, and he never corrected her, either because he was being polite by not correcting an adult or he couldn't really hear her over the cacophony of banging lumber and plastic. It was a bowling alley, and it was loud. It was around the same time as the stick figure war illustrations, but I didn't draw any while I was there. I was all business and chili dogs.

I only knew her town by name and what I'd read about it in annual "Worst Cities To Live" lists. I liked her, but not enough to visit her town. Besides, I had progressed to ping pong, four square, pinball, and arcade games. My bowling days were behind me.

My stick-figure-war-drawing days were behind me as well, but making cards afforded me the opportunity to express my artistic creativity and do so in the company of a cute, cool girl, so I was makin' me some Christmas cards!

I had other creative friends (I'm not counting Tully), and some had initially undertaken the holiday exercise as well, but as the night stretched on into the quiet, wee hours, the room thinned out. Eventually, it was just me sitting on the floor hunched over a bunch of magazine clippings, a few fistfuls of colored pencils, some markers, and a glue stick. Also scattered in a tight, reachable circle were countless sheets of every size and poundage of paper... and Alley. I chose a 5x7 section of card stock and moved closer to Alley, still respectful of the rings of pre-art.

She was allowing her creativity and artistic imagination to guide her hands, and the results were...surreal. That's the best way I found to describe something I know is art, but don't really understand the artistic value of. What she was creating was art. What I was doing was using her paper, colored pencils, pens, and markers to make festive shapes and intentionally hackneyed holiday statements, but I was concentrating and not even focusing on

Alley. Not focusing on Alley would have been considerably more difficult in nearly any other circumstance, but I was making art!

Alley was lithe. I had just learned that word, and it suited her perfectly. She wore thrift store house dresses that just sort of meandered around the bones that, when balanced as they were, made up her skeleton. She had a lean face that admitted she knew what you were up to and was now just waiting to see what you did next.

She commanded my attention without words or movements, and just existing as a cute, cool, effortlessly lovely girl would have been enough usually. Not now, for now I was an artist...in a beret... with a glue stick!

I selected and lined up a pallid green sheet of card stock, arranging the edge of the line of the paper with the line created by the far wall meeting the floor.

In the interest of brevity and the organization mandated by such a succinct undertaking, I will now document the remainder of steps as bullet points:

- I created, as the background of the card, a transitional grade from indigo to periwinkle with a colored pencil.
- I selected and outlined metallic dice with a fine point pen.
- I had previously typed and printed the words "Pair-A-Dice Lounge" from the university's computer lab.
- I cut the paper displaying the words "Pair-A-Dice Lounge" in half, so the words "Pair-A-Dice" and "Lounge" each have their own separate section of paper.
- I set aside those pieces of paper (unglued for now) next to the unfinished card.
- I procured a metal ruler and drew a rhombus in ink.

I rubbed the glue stick repeatedly on the rhombus and attached the pieces of paper displaying the words "Pair-A-Dice" and "Lounge" over each other, so it read, "Pair-A-Dice" on top of the word "Lounge."

This was the focal point of the card, along with a crude sketch of the actual brick and mortar lounge, also shaded to demonstrate depth. Whether or not the lounge is constructed with bricks and mortar is irrelevant—it's symbolic. Artists use symbols and metaphors...and wear berets. It gave the card legitimacy and me legitimacy as an artist, even more than the beret.

I pressed the paper against the sticky stripes of glue stick residue and solidified the bond with the side of a plastic card for/ from a bulk wholesale outlet where I purchased enough animal crackers for a military unit. (By the way, I don't think effective, intimidating military units eat animal crackers, but they could've.)

Hanging off the bottom of the "Pair-A-Dice Lounge" sign was a smaller sign announcing the lounge's festive, holiday spirit by declaring a "Merry Xmas to All." The L was falling off, so the sign was reduced to one that read "Merry Xmas to Al."

I was debating whether to either trace or fasten with rubber cement—which I also had access to—a few metallic silver stars on the sky behind the lounge. I opted to do neither because it made the card imbalanced and busy. Boy, I was thinking like a real artist!

During my satisfied pause, it became undeniably obvious how long we had been working on our cards. Alley had finished or abandoned her holiday card and finished two pieces of art. I has just finished my card when I heard the ROTC kids waking up and stretching before their pre-assigned workouts. I would get color copies of my card tomorrow to mail out to family and unrelated "family." My friends would get cards, even the artists, but their cards would be black and white.

With the paper neatly stacked, the rubber cement, glue stick, and markers capped, and the scissors and pencils separated and returned to either the shoe box or cigar box from which they came, I was liberated from the task of forging my version of "art." I could now embrace Alley as though we had just triumphantly completed a rigorous trail or won a race...or something else that mandated a hug. I wearily hugged her, and we kissed. She knew we were going to and had subtly and patiently worn me down over several hours. I could tell by her smile she knew we were going to kiss. I couldn't and didn't trust that smile, so I kissed it several more times.

XXXIV

Colleen doesn't really like me. I don't think Colleen really likes anyone. I mean, she might have liked people before me, but I would never dive into the "Colleen" end of the pool for fear I would hit my head on the bottom. She's shallow.

I don't see her falling deeply and truly in love with someone; someone who makes her life better, makes colors brighter, sounds richer, blah, blah, blah. I don't think she has or can experience deep, robust, true love. I don't feel this way just because she doesn't like me, which she doesn't. I'm just pretty insightful regarding such things. It's my opinion.

She is pretty, but pretty in the stereotypical blonde hair, blue-eyed way high school cheerleaders in movies and television shows are pretty. This grants her a license to be distant and cold. Well, I think she thinks it does. I'm merely speculating; it's probably sour grapes because she doesn't like me.

Her father, who I have never met and would probably be dismissed by because I don't play or care about American football, had been a professional football player. I have no documentation to back up my theory, but I'll bet she's spoiled, too. I've heard numerous accounts and read countless stories (well, at least two) about professional football players who played for years and now have nothing to show for it except spoiled kids and a head injury, but I'll bet she's spoiled mean. Again, I couldn't support my suspicions with facts or tangible evidence, but that doesn't make them any less palpable. Also, it might be sour grapes.

We were on our way to the company holiday party for the restaurant where we both worked when she came to pick me up at my apartment. We both work the door in the hostess/host capacity, so we only work together when I'm a barback and she is hosting. That's the only time I see her at all. She offered (or agreed) to pick me up and give me a ride to the festivities, but we wouldn't be sitting at the same table when the gift swap started. She doesn't like me.

She's pretty, in a stereotypical way, and we did kiss at my apartment, which she walked up several flights of stairs to get to when she came to pick me up, and she did sit a spell, as they say, when she got up there, but she's pretty empty...except for not liking me. That's a flushed-out opinion. She probably doesn't even have a well-defined reason why she doesn't like me either. It's probably my big ears or bent nose, and I had nothing to do with either of those. It's probably sour grapes though, because she doesn't like me.

When she ascended the three flights of stairs to my apartment, I was purposely underdressed for someone attending this type of social gathering because I wanted to announce I was changing and give her the opportunity to follow me into my room and kiss me while only partially dressed. That is, of course, if she wanted to. Plus, I had found and procured a polyester shirt with a massive sailboat on it so I could "change into something a little more comfortable." I was wearing it and would need to announce I had to "put on something nice for the party." It still granted her the chance to follow me and kiss me while I was changing. She did not. She didn't like me.

There were going to be scores of people whose opinions greatly mattered to me, and whose acceptance I was strenuously trying to gain. Those individuals had witnessed me dressed to the nines in my sequin shirt or black and white wingtips ("spectators," they're called), or tuxedo shirt with black fringe, all just to take names and quote waiting times in an environment so dimly lit no one could see me anyway. These social idols of mine were expecting me to make an entrance and collect envious glares (I hoped), but this girl, this diabetic arm candy, had no interest in curious stares or the man walking next to her. I'll bet she would have felt differently if she had any interest in me romantically... which she didn't.

When we were kissing, and my hands smoothed down her cashmere sweater (of course it was), I opened my eyes a few times and she was always looking over my shoulder, off into nothing like an actor playing a blind person. If she liked me, she would have kept her eyes closed and fought off a kiss-altering smile, but she didn't smile, because I don't think she likes me or anyone. She probably couldn't write an essay about it or give a speech on why she doesn't or didn't, but I doubt she is or was or would ever be pressured to do so. Pretty blonde girls don't have to give speeches or write essays, and if they do, and the speeches and essays are terrible, a much older man in a position of authority who probably thinks about her when he masturbates had or will tell her, "I see potential there!" or "That's a good point," when there isn't any potential and it isn't a good point.

XXXV

"So, I guess you got some girls liking you."

He was doing his best to appear either as an empathetic confidant or intimidating, and since I couldn't tell which one it was, he wasn't very intimidating.

"What's that mean? Who?"

"Just don't hurt anyone."

"I won't, thanks."

I wonder who he means. Was that a warning? Was it a threat? He isn't very threatening with that middle-school, glued-on chinstrap beard. Who does he mean? Stockton? She doesn't like me... well, only as a friend. Who "likes me?" Who am I going to hurt? I don't hurt anyone. I won't hurt anyone. I think he's friends with Krista, but she gave me quite a tongue-lashing (quite literally... ugh) before and after the dance we went to and I doubt that's who he meant. I don't know anyone else who likes me like that, and we don't exactly run in the same circles. Well, I thought we didn't.

His name is Nino, and we do play on the same high school soccer team. Well, I play, and he just sells drugs and steals shorts and stuff when we go as a team to the family-owned sporting goods store. The shorts are basically handkerchiefs made of parachute material, so they can (and are) easily stuffed into pockets and backpacks. The owners know and want to support members of local sports teams who will buy things they can't steal, like letterman jackets and shoes. The hoodlums like the kid who just warned/threatened me take it as a personal challenge to steal these forbidden items.

Then again, upon reevaluation, I think he might be talking about Amber. She was cute, but quiet. I suspect she was quiet because she wasn't the sharpest girl and was aware of herself enough to figure out if she didn't say a lot, no one could prove her intelligence (or lack thereof).

She lived in the shadow of her sister, the captain of the cheerleading squad and a real Barbie doll. I had only heard rumors, and I didn't pay much attention to rumors, especially if they dealt with legends of people, not the people themselves. These were the people whose last names were used every time they were the subject of rumors and alleged facts.

Her mother, for instance, had a drinking problem...maybe, that's just what I heard. Her mother was also single now, and I had never heard even whispers of a father present anywhere in her life. Amber could have told me her mother wasn't a drunk, or someone in my life closer to Amber's mother could have cleared her name, but I never asked, and the legend continued.

Amber used to be in the same grade as me, but that was a long time ago, back in first or second grade...I think. I was moved up in the middle of fourth grade, and she was held back. I was too busy being made fun of or chased home in sixth grade to remember when she was held back, but she wasn't in my world in fifth grade, sixth grade, freshman year, or even until very recently.

I was re-introduced to her through Jonas, who was a bad influence. I should accept some of the blame for letting myself be influenced, but he and his circle of friends were outside the circle of friends I previously spent my time with (the good, non-drinking, non-promiscuous, curfew-obeying, good kids), so they were exotic and mysterious. They were foreign to me and I'll admit, I was intrigued.

I had never stayed out gallivanting around long after the local news had concluded, and the syndicated television shows and infomercials began. I had stayed up late, but it was never out in public, and certainly never in someone my age's beat-up, booming, thumping, and rusty car. Well, I had now, and was present, not for the lewd events the stories dealt with, but for the laughing and telling and re-telling of stories about lewd events, and for the boisterous laughing and miming of the kid who was "sucking on titties like a baby" in the back seat. It wasn't the life I knew, so it was like watching a movie. Not a good movie, but a motion picture about a life I didn't live.

I think Amber was just born into her life like she was born into the shadow of a light she didn't ask for, just like she was born into an assumed reputation and the behavior that accompanied it. I don't recall ever hearing any blatant declarations about the looseness of her morals, but I'll admit, I was swayed by the character of the company she kept and the rumors of their transgressions.

Those rumors made me feel older than her (which I wasn't) and disingenuously bold (argumentative) while I was sitting on the couch where we were just kissing. Those rumors were also probably the catalyst for my premature, but successful, breast fondling. They were also most likely the reason when she got up to change, I impishly asked if she "needed any help" from the living room down the hall. I'm not exactly sure what "help" I could provide or why she would need it, but she declined so I didn't have to improvise.

She came to my soccer game and we sat in the back seat of my parents' enormous sedan on the way home. I scooted closer to Amber, while my mother showed off a folder of glossy pages demonstrating her aptitude as a professional consultant or technical writer or technical writing consultant or whatever title was on her business cards and emails. I didn't really understand what I was supposed to be impressed with or why Amber should care, but she quietly listened as my mother explained, successfully masking her ignorance yet again.

L (part 6)

I was anticipating Violet's visit and eagerly awaiting her arrival. I was imagining and re-imagining the time we would be spending together—what she would be wearing (or not wearing), the stories of her experiences, how she looked when she slept, ate, and sneezed. I was so excited for her, and just to be in her presence once again. She is dynamic, and her charisma, though more subtle than bombastic, was intoxicating. Also, it might have been the gin.

There was one glaring, nagging problem that haunted me about her guest appearance in my new life—I couldn't remember her face. She had silver hair, I knew that. It was impactful and had made its intended impression on me. I also knew she had tattoos, and since the state where me and my floppy, greasy pompadour now lived was experiencing a record number of consecutive days above 90 degrees, I doubted, with certainty, they wouldn't be covered up. I couldn't remember her face, but it might have been the gin.

I hadn't been in my new home long enough for it to be disheveled, and I worked as much as possible, so I wasn't present enough to create much of a mess (if you didn't count the vomit on the curtain, and I cleaned that up when I awoke the next morning). We had uniforms for my new job, and we were required to wear khaki pants, so I had a sizeable pile of dirty khaki pants, underpants, t-shirts, and socks, but not really a "mess." I routinely washed my cereal bowl after breakfast, the spoon I had used, and the knife I used to slice the one banana and four strawberries I had in my cereal. I had a regimen, and I was proud enough of it to share this otherwise intimate detail with anyone close enough to hear it.

The bathroom was the only moderately cluttered room in the apartment because of my frequent showering, and the fact I put so much time, effort, and products into my appearance. The suffocating humidity and the stink it provoked due to the sweat it provoked, provoked at least two showers a day. This meant there was perpetually a wet towel on the hook next to the sink. Sometimes, I put the wet towel on the bed, which was a poor decision because it made a damp spot on the blanket. Although the spot usually dried before I turned in for the night, and I was the only one laying on the dampness if it didn't, its moistness was acceptable. I would need to correct such behavior since I was not going to be the only occupant of my bed, a thought which made me the very best kind of nervous.

The Thursday afternoon Violet was set to arrive in the town where I lived(!) at the apartment where I lived(!), where she would be sleeping in my bed(!), I waited tables during the lunch shift. I told my co-workers ad nauseam about the existence of Violet, the plans I had once she arrived (though I was open to improvisation), and that I would see them tonight when I brought Violet in for dinner.

With a proud, beaming smile, I told them all about her silver hair and tattoos. They oohed and aahed, and I tried ineffectively to give the impression it was no big deal. It was, though, a very big deal. I was told repeatedly, "North Carolina has girls, too. You don't need to import them."

"Not like this one," I responded. "Not like this one."

To be continued...

Nicholas J. Stevens

XXXVI

What I was doing I wouldn't call "sitting," but I was distraught. So, I was positioned upside-down in a utilitarian dorm room chair silently lamenting over the fact that Jodi had not one, but multiple hickeys on her neck. None were mine.

These hickeys were intentional hickeys, not the accidental "ooh, I'm really attracted to you and I really like kissing you and can't even...whoops! Teehee" kind of hickeys. These were the "you're hot and I'm gonna mark my territory/I'm so wasted" kind of hickey. They were intentional hickeys. They were the kind of indigo stamps that spurn inverted melancholy. So, here I was.

Jodi and I attended the last orientation session for incoming freshmen, and it coincided and ran into the commencement of the school year. I felt like a rebellious wild child because a girl stayed overnight in my room before the school year even started and, more importantly, before my roommate moved in.

Jodi was pretty, and pretty thin. She had long, straight, walnut hair that flowed over her diminutive shoulders and the slight points of her breasts. She didn't wear a bra, and not out of female rebellion; she just didn't need to. The weathered, oversized Grateful Dead t-shirt she was wearing enveloped her, and had not been white in what appeared to be a very long time, but still contrasted starkly from the violet of the hickeys.

Her face was pale and drawn and her mouth was nothing more than a slit. This gave her a perpetual bashful, but confused look. I could personally attest to the fact that she was not at all bashful, but Jarvis' multiple mouth prints on her neck announced it loudly, so I never had to. The nebulous crew we assembled as budding friends didn't ask and wouldn't care anyway.

Regarding Jarvis, he was more her type in every way than I was. He wore old (or at least they looked old) elephant leg jeans that had multiple tears visible when he played hacky sack, which he did constantly when he wasn't forcefully sucking on Jodi's neck. I am certain the tears in his jeans didn't result from any activity more strenuous than the hacky sack or smoking weed.

He was ratty and had a literal mop of hair that was too lazy to stretch down to his shoulders. He liked smokin' weed and drinkin' 40s, and probably anything else that rescued him from the confinement of young, white, intentional stupidity.

They were meant for each other, either long enough to give and receive hickeys or for the long haul. Jodi and I were not. She used my toothbrush, we slept next to each other, we kissed (on the mouth, so no hickeys were produced), and I got a dirty, old t-shirt and a reputation.

The situation had become clear to me, so I up-righted myself in the utilitarian dorm chair, I resigned to learn nothing at all, and I moved on to the next failed attempt at lasting romance.

XXXVII

Bionca was a punk girl, too cool to date me
My words, not hers, she didn't care enough to rate me
I'm excited by her "difference"
And I like her purple hair
She introduces me to records
And to dare, bare, and gasp for air
She grabs the back of my head, and never says, "Please"
She just forces it down in between her open knees
I never object, and absorb her teachings
My joy matches her joy, laughing, and screeching
She invited me to a party where everyone wore just underwear,
With their clothing now gone, I imagined what was
under there
I tried like hell to hide my arousal
But it was hard (pun intended), good thing there was carousal
She sat across the room in a chair, just observing
I did "private things" as she click clacked her tongue
stud; unnerving
We listened to her boyfriend(?) on the university station
She would respectfully turn it down in times of elation
She invited an old friend to my dormitory
Like so much of Bionca, it became quite reforming
Her friend was a skinhead, complete with the skinhead buzz
I thought that meant Nazi before I knew what a skinhead was
Her friend liked ska music and working-class pride
My comment "ignorance isn't bliss" was clearly not justified

I was shamed this time, but not for very long
I tried to be ostentatious, but I was clearly just very wrong
Bionca is awesome and a force in my growing
Between dating, loving, and exploring, I'll gladly keep toeing.

XXXVIII

The chalkboard on the right side of Mrs. Handler's classroom is littered with "Batboy loves #7 loves Batboy loves #7...loves Batboy loves #7" and was repeated up and down and across it in different, but similar colors and fonts. It was obvious that two people had written the words, the alternating lines, and the declarations of "love" they knew nothing about.

I'm Batboy. I'm Batboy because, to shake off the identity of someone who is either ignored completely or ridiculed and chased home, I have engulfed myself in everything Batman and have adopted the persona of a Batfan...actually, the biggest Batfan. I'm "Batboy!"... who loves #7 who loves...you understand)

I have: a Batman baseball hat (covered with well over 30 Batman pins of all shapes and sizes); a Batman painter's hat; Batman Converse All Star sneakers (they make Joker ones, too, and although I like them and understand the importance of the existence of The Joker, I have the Batman ones); wristbands; socks; Batman cereal (that came with a plastic Batman logo bowl); Batman figurines; countless Batman comic books (from well before the movie was released and the official comic book of the movie); and countless other memorabilia and collectables.

I have worn a Batman t-shirt every single day of the school year except picture day, when my parents made me wear a ridiculous, hideous cardigan. I have five Batman shirts, so it's not gross. I look forward to long weekends, so I can wear the four I like most. I would wear that fluorescent print one with the Joker on it, but I eliminate it from the rotation if given the opportunity.

Cera is "#7" because she wears the number seven on the soft-ball team. I don't think anyone calls her "#7," but I understand whose graffiti it is and who "loves" me, so it makes enough sense, and it's cute.

I don't know if I would or could call it "love." I mean, I like her, but I more just agreed to be her boyfriend rather than pursued her as my girlfriend. It was more romantic and serious than my first girlfriend, last year (if you don't count Brandy, who I played that plastic hippo board game with back in preschool). I never kissed Brandy, or my girlfriend last year, Wendy.

Wendy and I would just give each other notes and say hello when we passed in the hall. She was in eighth grade, and I was already younger because I skipped a grade, so I was a year behind her, and my birthday is in late May, so I was even younger by school standards. I invited her to join me for soccer games and be involved in my fake responsibilities at the community theatre my mom ran, but we never kissed or anything. When it came time for her to break it off and commence high school, I don't think either of us was heartbroken. I know I wasn't heartbroken, and what we had never grew into more than a relationship in name anyway.

That was before Cera, and before we kissed in the hallway next to the metal lockers at school, my first kiss. The hall monitor was slacking off somewhere, so I don't think anyone would have seen us.

I liked it. It was soft and we both laughed a little afterwards. It was like a verbal blush, and it might have been her first kiss too, I'm not sure. We were in middle school, so we were supposed to know about people the other person had dated or whatever, but she had gone to a different grade school, so I wouldn't know the faces attached to the names anyway.

Like Wendy and I, Cera and I held hands, but we seized the opportunity to kiss. I also told her I wanted to take a shower with her, and that was a recurring fantasy of mine. Like most fantasies

I entertained, I was intrigued by the idea of the situation, but the characters and setting never flourished into actions.

I didn't really know what in the world I would have done if she had agreed to my hypothetical suggestion, but she never did, so I didn't have to deal with it, and wasn't forced to make decisions I saw as pre-ordained.

On the topic of fantasies, in the room where Mrs. Handler edified scores of students on literary matters and two star-crossed... likers" declared their liking on the chalkboard, we were visited by a student teacher who made it very uncomfortable and embarrassing for boys in middle school to go to the chalkboard (because she is beautiful and made them grow erections). She was gorgeous.

She and I had a connection based on drawings of soccer shoes I had created and given to her, for no apparent or relevant reason. She had liked them, and I pined for her approval and acceptance, so I drew as many as my unskilled hands could offer.

They were, if kept (and I was certain they were), confined to a bag with all the other collections of papers that would be ignored and/or rarely referenced once she graduated and secured a permanent teaching position. I wanted to, and did, believe that I was thought about and worthy of a surprised smile if my name came up in discussions or her experiences in Mrs. Handler's class.

One afternoon, near the conclusion of her time spent with us (I made no assumptions about the two being related), she arrived in the classroom clearly flummoxed about something she had witnessed or seen on the way there. These suspicions were confirmed as she told the captive audience details of what had transpired.

"Oh my God! Oh my God!"

She did not wait for nor require encouragement to continue with her story.

"There was a fight, two women fighting and screeching and pulling hair, and it was... then one called the other a 'cum dumpster!'"

The class was frozen in the suspended animation of shock and awe. It was not a phrase I had heard before, and not in the lexicon of the garden variety eighth grader she said it to. It was the honors class, so no kids from "the other side of the tracks" who might know or have ever used the term were in the class and were not currently present.

She realized, as soon as she heard the words leave her perfect lips and saw the blank faces that had heard her and were stricken speechless, that she had just said and thus introduced "cum dumpster" to a room full of eighth graders.

"Don't tell anyone I said that." I strongly doubted anyone could obey her if they wanted to, which I doubted even more anyone wanting to.

"Actually, just forget I ever said that." It was beyond doubting, and I knew I would never, could never, forget.

L (part 7)

My apartment building was in a cluster of identical apartment buildings at the end of a long road lined with and under a canopy of tall trees. The leaves of those trees shaded you and waved in the breeze, but it was so high up you wouldn't normally notice it. The road constituted the end of the walk home, and the shade offered welcome amnesty from the aggressive sunlight.

Violet was driving towards me under the curtain of those trees, and we both smiled ear to ear when we saw, and instantly recognized, the other's face. I didn't want or need leaves to screen her beaming. She stopped to let me into her car, where we exchanged insignificant details about her drive and the patrons I waited on that day. She drove me the block and a half back to my door, which provided evidence she had already been there, and unnecessarily explained she had already been there. There was a note on the door that read, "Went for a drink and a pony ride." I apologized for interrupting her plans (for a pony ride) and offered to buy her a drink and look for a farm. She agreed to the drink, but said she had a surprise for me. She had a box under one arm, and the bag with her toiletries and clothes in the other. I felt an inflated sense of accomplishment about her assumption that she was sleeping over, even though we had discussed it numerous times, and it had evolved past the point of being awkward or polite. It was a given at this juncture, and only logistics were addressed like where things were to be placed, and if I had any ice or not.

In the box, my "surprise" was a pair of glistening stainless-steel silver cocktail glasses. I thanked her and poured us black drinks consisting predominantly of Sambuca. It complimented the shiny metallic glasses, the inky beverages, and the silver piercings in her ears and face. It didn't matter how many times or hours we had spoken on the telephone or the level of comfort we enjoyed—I was nervous, the very best kind of nervous, the kind layered with excitement and fascination.

We mutually agreed to have dinner at the restaurant & microbrewery where I worked and had left only hours before. We chose table 203, which overlooked ostensibly the main and only street in town. I had buttermilk fried chicken with mashed potatoes and green beans, and she had stout-marinated pork chops with mashed sweet potatoes and a braised leafy green vegetable I was not familiar with.

There were more drinks involved, and I was not aware of or giving much attention to the fact there had been proofed beverages for every step of our growing romance. Had I been cognizant of this revelation, I would have referenced the results of a marriage study I heard on public radio. It stated most divorced couples, a solid majority, separated because one partner believed the other drank too much. This was not the only common sense I ignored.

To be continued...

XXXIX

The phone rattled. It was Sascha, inviting me out to a bar I could not enter were it not for Will's drivers license. Will looked enough like me to be in the same police lineup, but couldn't take my place at family events, even if the events were thrown for and attended by the older members of the family. All the numbers—which I suspected was all anyone who possessed authority to make decisions at the bar looked at—were acceptable. Sascha sometimes worked as a DJ, sometimes as a drummer, sometimes as a baker, a designer, an artist, sometimes as an ingenue, sometimes as a muse (which must be exhausting) and sometimes, Sascha did not work at all. She had done something brilliant and popular at that bar and had photographic identification, so the guardians at the entrance were accepting, even encouraging, of her presence.

I excused myself to speak to Sascha privately, away from Aurora.

"Yeah. Yeah, I have it. I can't, I'm in the bathroom and the fan's on. No! I'm not going to the bathroom right now, I just have the fan on. I just don't want her to hear me. No, it's fine. Yeah, I've used it there before and no one cares. No, you're fine. Yes, she's still here. No, not really. No, I don't. I know, I really want to see them, too! Okay, you still have the car? No, I'll take care of it. I'll make something up. No, it's fine, really. Give me, like, 20 minutes. Yeah, that would be great. I'll be downstairs in 20."

She was *slightly, loosely*, draped in the clothing she wore over.

"Do I want what? Like oral sex? I never heard that term before. Heh," I chuckled uncomfortably. "Um, no thank you? I really have to go. Our friend is not doing well, I guess. No, my friend just told me. Apparently, a co-worker of mine 'tried' acid again, and they're losing their shit. Sorry, but I gotta go. No, thank you. Sorry, but this needs to be tended to. No, thank you, though, I gotta go."

Nicholas J. Stevens

XL

Luna was a pioneer, a rebel without effort or intention.

She was part of the loose collective of friends unofficially known as "The Kindergarten Crew," deemed so for their propensity to indulge in sophomoric behavior.

She wore shin-length cargo shorts, or shin-height cargo pants, depending on where you started, and appeared to have been dressed in them by whatever toy manufacturer had made the action figure that was her. She wore once-white skate shoes too, and they were also part of her designated outfit, though I don't recall ever seeing her ride a skateboard. I remember her carrying one a few times, but I think it was more of an accessory rather than childish transportation to the next giggling activity. She has a congregation of curls lazily falling over sparkling eyes that grew wide with the excitement of youthful exuberance over kickball, puffy stickers, or a shiny thing.

Luna was present for that night's four square game, which we took very seriously, despite generally being reserved to elementary school playgrounds. The chosen location for this and similar events was "The Porch" outside the freshmen dorm towers. The Porch was a collection of small, smooth stones sealed together with cement. It was sectioned off into square segments, and, thus, perfect for a four square court (or several). It had become ringed by those waiting for their turns, those mourning eliminations, and those spectators brave enough to venture a closer look at the action and unintentionally volunteer for an impromptu game of dodgeball.

The rules were simple. Actually, the rules started simple, but were mutated and distorted by the present King (that is the individual who had advanced to the King position by defeating players 2, 3, and 4, or by avoiding elimination when they were eliminated by another player). The King got to call rules, which changed as new kings entered the hallowed King square and began their reign. Rules could be created or enacted according to the king's whim.

The rules were called Natural Disasters, like Earthquakes (where a player was allowed to grab the ball with both hands, jump into the air, and land on two feet while slamming the ball on the ground as forcefully as possible while yelling, "Earthquake!"), Tornadoes (where a player cupped the ball between his curved palm and forearm while spinning around before skipping the ball through another player's square, all while yelling, "Tornado"), and Volcanoes (wherein the player yells, "Volcano!", and grabs the ball, similar to an Earthquake, but throws the ball as high into the air as possible. It was, in my opinion, the least effective Natural Disaster as well as the riskiest since the ball could simply miss the court on the return decent, and the player who called it eliminated themselves in the process). There was a great deal of yelling in our games of four square.

I like to call "Le Roi" (the French King), which requires a player to yell a French word, any word, before or as they strike the ball. With the mono-lingual nature of most of the players, tasking them to think of and pronounce a French word to accompany their game plan allowed for a greater degree of me eliminating them. I think they get overwhelmed. They were not used to thinking about things that weren't related to the game while the game was going on.

"Trees" was another popular (and effective) category for a King to call. In addition to knocking out, or eliminating, numerous players, it spawned a bevy of nicknames. The most notable was Benny Poplar, who took other players and onlookers by surprise and crippling hilarity when he called, "Poplar!" during a match. It was funny because no one expected it to come from him, and because his familiarity with dendrology was underestimated, it immediately became his nickname. Thus, Benny Poplar was born.

I had just gotten knocked out when I struggled to produce a French word (even though je parle beaucoup de François!) and playing the ball in bounds, simultaneously. The crowd groaned, then clapped to signal their appreciation and respect of my play and tenure as Le Roi. I shook my head and sulked to the end of what had become a lengthy line.

Luna was hugging goodbyes to various members of the line and was heading off to another childish activity that would have been a very tempting affair if there was not currently an intense four square competition taking place, which there was. Her anticipation of whatever was next incited her more rapid advance through the tail end of line.

When Luna reached the fin de la ligne, she reached me, still distraught about my French language failing, and reached out to grasp the sides of my face like a player grasping the ball attempting an Earthquake. As quickly and carelessly as one would lackadaisically high five a victorious acquaintance, she kissed me on the lips. She was smiling and distracted, and I was left kissed and open-jawed, forgetting about my elimination and pretty much everything else.

XLI

HT – her thoughts, HW – her words
MT – my thoughts, MW – my words

HT: What the fuck am I doing? Did I just get picked up? Ugh, what the fuck? I think I just got picked up What am I doing? Why in the hell would I go back to his place?!? I've got to be safer! He's probably a serial killer! Well, if he is, he's not a very good one At least, he isn't very sneaky He's always at the same place, combing his hair.

MT: What am I doing? Can I just work slingin' coffee, and just come home and watch a movie or something? Do I always have to be picking up chicks? Did I really just call them "chicks?"

HT: Well, I'm not doing anything to him I just came from the gym, and I'm wearing my "period panties." No one is ever supposed to actually see them. No one is ever going to see them, especially not this Elvis wannabe! The panties are gross and blood-stained, and I'm wearing them because I was just going to the gym, and then I got picked up by this guy. If I have my period panties on, he's not going to see me in them! And unless he's a sicko, he shouldn't want to see them, let alone take them off, which I'm not letting him do. Sorry sicko, I need to do laundry

MW: "Do you want something to drink or something? I don't really have any food. I think there are some chips and guacamole, but…"

HW: "Do you have any beer?"

MW: "No. I have whiskey and gin and stuff."

MT: ...which is nothing like beer, Stevens. Pull it together.

HW: "Is there a state store nearby? I don't know this neighborhood really well."

MT: You don't know English "really well," either. That wasn't very nice. She's nice, and cute. She didn't deserve that. Be nice.

HW: "You work at that Mexican place too, don't you? Are you always working? What else do you do?"

HT: ...besides pick up innocent, dumb girls and sniff period panties.

MW: "I play pinball a lot and ride my bike and...I don't know, that's about it. I work a lot."

HW: "And pick up unsuspecting girls at the coffee shop?"

MW: "Just the cute ones."

MT: I'll just flash a smile and move a little closer.

MW: "Hi."

HT: "Hi?" I am not fucking this guy! He's...he's awfully close! I'll kiss him, maybe, but he's not sniffing my period panties, sicko. I wonder what he'll do if I mess up his hair? Let's see.

MT: Whoa! Stay away from the hair, sugar! I just combed it...extensively. I do want to kiss her, and I do want to touch her skin. I want to touch her waist and the small of her back. She's cute. She's fit.

MW: "What did you do at the gym? Like, do you have different days for different body parts?"

HW: "Today was back. I was on the erg mostly. Do you know what that is? Like, the rowing machine? I did a bunch of squats too, and lunges. Do you work out?"

HT: I'm not fucking him, and he's not smelling my panties.

MW: "I do. I also get a lot of exercise at work, the other work, like when I barback. I have to get ice from the basement, and I do curls with the ice buckets before I come back up. They're heavy. And there are stairs too, so that's something. I ride my bike quite a bit. I rode in that bike ride for MS or whatever, like, up to Lake

Erie. It was 150 miles in two days, and I don't have 'slicks' (the tires) so I rode the whole thing on knobby tires. It's harder. I rode in the other one too, up the hill with the incline. Like the ski lift incline, not just that it's on an incline. I know about the erg, too. I like them. My friend was on her rowing team in college in Ohio, and she introduced me to it. I like them."

MT: I want to kiss her. I want to put my hand on her body, on the small of her back. I bet it's tight. I bet you can feel the muscles underneath, like, the muscles she worked out today.

MW: "Do you want to watch something? Do you like this show? This is one my favorite episodes. Johnny Cash is in this one. He's the voice of the coyote.

HW: "I don't know. I don't watch TV. I study a lot, and train."

MW: "For what? Do you play a sport?

HW: "Olympic lifting."

MW: "You were in the Olympics?!?...or are you going to be?"

MT: Oh my god, I want to see her in her underwear! I'll bet it's awesome! I want to...caress her and kiss her in her underwear. I want to feel skin against skin. I want to kiss her and touch her.

HW: "No, power lifting. I just train it for me, not competitively for anything. Do you have vodka?"

MW: "Oh, and I play soccer for a class and I want to walk on to the university team. A couple guys I play with are on the university team, and they said I can probably walk on. I've played since I was four, both outdoor and indoor. My senior year of high school, I led the indoor team in goals and penalty minutes. Pretty badass."

HW: "Why are you taking a class? If you're good enough to be on the team, what are you learning in the class? Do you have any vodka?"

MW: "Well, I mean it's not really to learn anything. It's just to play and meet other people who play."

HW: "Are other people in your class good?"

MW: "Well, not as good as the guys on the team or me, but it's good to play the guys on the team, and to be scheduled to play, like, to have to."

HW: "I don't get it. Seems like a waste. Why don't you play intramurals? Those are scheduled."

MW: "I do! Our team, The Machine, is actually in the fraternity league, so we get to beat up frat boys!"

HW: "You're in a fraternity? You don't seem like a frat boy."

HT: If he's in a fraternity, I'm definitely not fucking him! I'm not getting fucking date raped, either! What kind of guy is in a fraternity? That's gross.

MW: "No, no, no! I am very much not in a fraternity. I would never be. I told my roommates that the first time I met them, last year. I lived with, like, five of them in a suite. They were all in the same frat, and I told them first thing I wasn't joining their frat, and I wasn't going to do shit because I was a freshman and they were all sophomores."

HW: "You lived with five frat brothers in a suite? That sounds awful and gross. Do you have any vodka?"

MW: "Yeah. And yeah, but it's a really nice bottle I was saving for a special occasion or something, like a celebration or anniversary or something special. I don't know, like a 'thing.' You know?"

HW: "Are you married? Whose anniversary? Can I have a glass? Do you have soda or cranberry juice or something?"

MW: "The vodka's not open, but I don't have any cranberry juice anyway. I was saving it for a special occasion. Both the gin and the tonic are open, and I have limes, lemons, and mandarin oranges if you want one...or several."

HW: "What do you do with the mandarin oranges?"

HT: I'm not making a fucking fruit salad! And "several?" I am not fucking this guy!

MW: "I put them on gin and tonics, or gin cocktails, like martinis or something. Yesterday, I flushed a banana peel down the toilet. Do you want a cocktail with gin in it? I can put a mandarin orange segment on it for you." Wink.

HW: "No. Wait, what? Why did you flush a banana peel down the toilet?"

MW: "I had to go to the bathroom, and I was eating a banana. Not during going to the bathroom—I was still holding the peel. I had just taken out the garbage, and I don't use a lot of garbage, so I didn't want it to rot and stink in there. I've flushed an apple core before, too."

HT: What the fuck?! He's a total fucking strange-o. Yeah, nice, and cute in a '50s Halloween costume kind of way. But the goddamn mandarin oranges and the banana peel! What's with the mandarin oranges?!? I'm not going to kiss him. I mean, if he kisses me, I'll kiss him, but what the fuck? What does he have, like a fruit fetish? Is he going to try and fuck me with a frozen banana? Where's my vodka? I swear to God, though, if his face smells like panties, I'm going home. I don't know exactly where I am, but I think I saw a bus stop out front.

MT: She's really cute, and she smells good. I love the smell of female body odor, the kind that came from working out, not the crust punk not showering kind, the kind that smells like a woman. I have an affinity for the smell of woman. I'm going to lean in and...

HW: "Hey, I never got a drink. I was promised mandarin oranges."

MW: "I like the way you smell. I like you."

HT: You like the smell of my panties too, sicko.

MT: I'm going to slide my hand around the small of her back exposed between the bottom of her damp t-shirt and the apex of her peeking underpants. She likes that idea, right? Her back does feel good.

MW: "Mmm...You don't need mandarin oranges. You taste nice."

HW: "Is that a bus stop out front?"

Nicholas J. Stevens

HT: I know it is.

MW: "It is. Are you going?"

HW: "Yeah. I have to get up early, and I still have to do laundry and study."

HT: Sorry, buddy, but I'm doing all my laundry, panties too, you sick, handsome fuck.

MW: "Well, let me walk you out."

HW: "I can find my way downstairs. I can find my way to the bus stop too."

MW: "It's not a far walk, like back into town. I walk to the coffee shop and to the Mexican place. The people on the bus usually stink, too. One more for the road?"

MT: I'll kiss her again, this time with more passion—deeper, and for longer. I have a feeling this will be my last chance to do so, so I'll slide my hand down her back, farther, and down between her still-damp cotton underwear and her well-worked, tight buttocks.

Yes, I thought the word "buttocks." Seemed appropriate.

HT: He just slid his hands down my underwear! Down my soggy underwear! He's probably going to jerk off while he smells his hands. Wrong side, bucko!

HW: "Okay, goodbye. I'll walk."

L (part 8)

After dinner, we went to an underground bar down the street. It was not seedy or nefarious, nor secret in any way; it was actually below street level.

It was called "hell," and it was decorated with all manner of campy, devil-themed toys, signs, and figurines. They even had an older pinball machine with a demonic character on the backglass, and a circular area of the playfield that spun and sent the ball rapidly in random directions. I played this particular machine many times, and it was entertaining, but that's not what tonight was. Tonight, the focus was Violet.

We played a few games, and my ability to play pinball inexplicably seemed to improve when I imbibed gin and tonics. (I decided that was the correct plural form of gin and tonic, not gins and tonics because the drink was produced by the combination of one type of gin and one type of tonic. Thus, "gin and tonic" was the complete name for a singular drink and adding an "s" to the tail end made it plural.).

Violet could not declare the same heightened-when-intoxicated skill level. She was much cuter than I was, even with my sky-high pompadour and rolled up jeans and sleeves, so in my mind (and other parts of my body), her inferior play was acceptable. Plus, I had been playing for about 15 years.

There was a red vinyl couch not necessarily next to the pinball machine, but alone on the outskirts of the common area. It was across the bar from the devil-themed arcade games, and its location was center stage on the nonexistent stage, and spot-lit those who sat on it appearing to rest before or after a command performance (held only their fantasies). Violet and I took a seat on the couch, and most certainly appeared to fill the roles of those backstage superstars. We were asked more than once if we were in a band, and we suspiciously denied it. It was noticeably flattering, and those who excitedly asked insisted we were famous.

We sat together on the muted cherry red couch and held hands in the glow of a ringing and rattling Mephistopheles. We were sitting close, and I didn't have to lean over far to kiss her. I had been admiring her full lips, button nose, and small teeth all day, and in my dreams for the weeks prior.

Despite having a fervent imagination, I could have never foreseen how prophetic and ominous it would be to have our first kiss on a red leather couch in "hell." If this scene were in a romantic comedy (or tragedy) that someone else was watching while I was in the room, its hackneyed, clichéd fabrication would have been met with a sigh and deep eye roll.

We finished our plastic cup cocktails and adjourned back to my apartment to most likely have more, but this time from the shiny steel chalices Violet had given to me.

To be continued...

XLII

Wondering, bright-eyed
We kissed, her jean shorts were loose
Hands found hidden skin.

XLIII

We explored and kissed
On the phone with her boyfriend
I felt terrible.

XLIV

She had a nice twang
She could kiss with that mouth, too
Couldn't taste the twang.

XLV

Sascha is a model. Sascha is tall, lean, muscular, beautiful, and inherently fascinating. Pretty much *all* of my friends agree she is beautiful, so it must be true. She is not necessarily *my* cup of tea; our relationship was platonic at most. But, I acknowledge and agree with the popular consensus.

She got me a gig modeling (I don't know why I say that like I'm someone I'm not). It was actually *several* gigs promotional modeling. I didn't have to be Sascha's type of good looking because the jobs consisted of handing out free stuff and wearing a promotional t-shirt they provided. I gave out individually-wrapped sticks of gum; t-shirts that were similar but not the same as the one I was required to wear; I rebounded basketballs from a set of hoops attached to a truck trailer; and I rode on the back of a bladeless riding lawn mower driven by kids who paid absolutely no attention when I explained how to safely operate it. It had a kill switch (an unfortunate name) which I could press and make the wheels stop turning and motor stop running if the kid driving it went too far off course or headed towards a parked car.

Once, I wore a giant suit designed to make me look like an enormous walking hockey puck. It was poorly designed because if the person inside—in this case me—let their arms dangle, they went numb. I was more upset I couldn't comb my hair, but I don't think the designers cared about that. Also, it looked plush, but was not plush. That is a dangerous combination of traits when the human being inside desires not to be shoved around by the patrons of the bar carrying the alcohol being promoted. The giant puck was, again, not plush, and had a wooden frame skeleton. It was rigid and acted accordingly when pushed. It was a rough night.

Sascha was dating a girl who looked like she would be dating Sascha, or at least someone who did or wanted to look like her, if there were such a creature. Raven was long and svelte and had silken blonde hair that fell across her cheeks and perfect chin, but there just wasn't anyone around who looked like Sascha, even for the promotional events staffed by models who weren't hired for enough "print work." Raven, privately and proudly, silently rejoiced in their partnership. She flaunted Sascha.

I never saw them argue, but I got the impression—and it was based on nothing that existed in reality (but probably skewed by my adoration of and fascination with Sascha)—that Sascha didn't feel the same way Raven felt. I felt like she was wondering who was next and what kind of partner would make her feel the best kind of nervous. What being would be a formidable partner for Sascha?

We lived in a bad neighborhood in a lousy part of town where it was unfortunate, but not much of a surprise, when Sascha's bike was stolen from the porch when she went inside to retrieve a towel to wipe it down, and was interrupted by a phone call that delayed her for only long enough for someone to steal the bicycle and flee the scene.

We were across the street from a bodega that exclusively featured items labeled "NOT FOR INDIVIDUAL SALE" that were released from the confines of their boxes and relabeled and priced with a black marker. The selling of these items was arguably the least illegal activity within the security-camera-screen-shot-pho-to-laden walls of this little market. Did the managers, if there were any, really need to instruct customers to contact the authorities if someone wearing a ski mask entered the store? Would anyone who would be a patron of the little sanctum of sin actually contact the police about anything? Sascha did when her bike was stolen, but the investigation never investigated beyond writing down her name, the date, and the time of day. They glanced at the porch where the burglary had taken place, the scene of the crime, when they came into the apartment to commence the questioning. There was no back door, so they must have passed it on the way out too. I don't know if they looked again.

Raven and I didn't talk all that much, at least when I was awake. I'm not being fresh; according to her—and I didn't and don't remember any of it taking place—but we had a conversation when my mattress was placed in front of the French doors of Sascha's room, and she passed by it on the way in. She said I "sounded kind of weird" and "a little out of it." Apparently "it" was consciousness, and I was out of it. I was dead asleep.

Bunk beds were eventually set up in my room with a small couch placed beneath. I like to really put an emphasis on the *love*-part of it when I refer to my *loveseat*. It is also usually trailed by a wink, and I am wholly aware how ridiculous I sound, but I relish my ridiculousness and consider it part of my charm.

I encountered Raven only slightly less after her and Sascha broke up. By that point, she and I were no longer living together, and we had a falling out regarding money. She and Raven were going to get an apartment together, then they broke up. I had already agreed to live with Will in a much better apartment in a much better area, down the street from the rich people strip of shops. Sascha had broken up with Raven before they moved in together, and she still owed me money because I moved out and on.

I ran into Raven a few days before I moved again, this time to North Carolina, and this time with no scheduled return date. I had run into Raven a few times in those final days, and she had been trying to fix me up with her friend who either was a mime or just named after one. I was not interested.

Raven saw that we ran into each other several more times before I left. This time I *am* being fresh, and she took me back to her apartment.

Our clothes, which had been pressed and tucked and arranged perfectly, were now a metaphorical trail of bread crumbs leading to her bed. Naked, smooth, and warm, she asked, "Do you want to...?"

I said, "I don't," without feeling the need to explain I didn't really want to do that with anyone, and I had really upset several previous girlfriends because it's unheard of that any guy would not want to. I was waiting for the first and the last and maybe the only. I was fine with that. I think I was the only one content with that. We kissed and messed around, but I don't think Raven was as content with my contentment.

L (part 9)

We would have decided we were officially going steady, but no one has referred to dating exclusively as "going steady" in many decades, certainly not in our lifetimes. We did decide we were boyfriend and girlfriend or hooked up or seeing each other or going out or whatever term was currently being used to declare we were exclusively dating each other.

We decided this on Thursday, and we were officially dating all day Friday. Right now, Saturday, we each had cocktails, and lay on the carpet and linoleum that lined the dining room and kitchen in my new apartment. We laid head-to-head, facing opposite directions, and the carpet was soft, but firm, and still smelled like the industrial antiseptic cleaner the superintendent used to sterilize after the former tenant's exodus.

"You want to get married?"

I previously had no desire to commit myself or my life to another human being prior to this point, but I had fallen, and done so very hard, for the woman inches from my cheek.

"What?" She heard me, but disbelief made her ask for it again.

"Do you want to get married? To me?"

We were still laying on the carpet and linoleum but turned to face each other so we could see eyes and mouths when her mouth said, "I do." We kissed again, but this time I was kissing my fiancé for the first time.

When our hearts stopped pounding with the force of love and promise and excitement and eager commitment, she handed the phone to me, so I could call my parents. I wanted them in attendance for the ceremony, which we didn't know any details of, and I determined they would almost certainly want to know of my engagement. Her parents had not been together in years, but she wanted to inform them of our eventual betrothal in hopes their individual plans and wishes imitated those of my parents. My parents were still married, had been for decades, and did not represent the actions or emotions of most other married couples. They were always supportive of me (even when I was doing absurd, impractical, passionate things, which I was currently). Hers were not.

"Dad! I'm getting married!"

"Oh, yeah? How's the weather down there?"

"Yeah, it's hot. I'm getting married!"

"Yeah. How's your new job? Do you like the owner?"

"Dad, put Mom on the phone."

I proceeded to tell my mother about my exciting news, and the life-altering plans that followed. Actually, I didn't know any of the plans, and wouldn't be moving, so the news "I'm getting married!" was really all I had, at least for now.

"Yes. Yeah, she came to visit. Yeah, I know! She came to visit a record company in Carrboro! Yes, apparently there is. I don't know, I guess it's cheaper or something. Hey, I'm getting married!"

I suppose if I knew anything about where the ceremony was going to take place, when it was taking place, or what exactly our plans were afterwards, it would have been a more interesting declaration. For now, it sounded hypothetical, like it was something I decided I would partake in at an undetermined future time. But that was not the case! I was going to be married to Violet, and we were going to be a married couple who lived in love until death did us apart.

Truthfully, I had not learned, and did not know a great deal about Violet. I spoke to her often, and at great length prior to her arrival, but much of her time spent in North Carolina was done so tipsily on romantic enamoration or Sambuca. I didn't know if she had a middle name or what it was, and I didn't know the names of her parents, who were invited to the wedding, but whose attendance could not be guaranteed.

The interview at the record company went "very well," though not as well as our utopian visit, date, and kisses. Comparing anything to those is considerably unfair because they were just about as good as a visit, date, and kisses had ever been or ever will be.

We discussed the necessary, but jovial task of defining the particulars of our joining (not that way, though those would be taking place on the same day fiscally). After examining a calendar, we saw there was a Friday the 13th (what could be cooler?) a month and a half away. This would allow me to become more settled in my domicile, and her to go back to Pittsburgh to "tie up loose ends."

One of the loose ends she was "tying up" was the boyfriend she still had. He was not amused to meet me when I flew up to surprise her in the month and a half hiatus between our engagement and actual marriage. She informed him of my existence and our plans, but I did not find out his existence or their relationship for several years into our marriage when it did not and would not have altered anything.

We were and are both considerable fans of Frank Sinatra and had an affinity to the song "South Of The Border," which afforded an opportunity for a humorous, but charming choice of a marriage venue. The American roadside attraction was not what Sinatra was singing about, but it was called South Of The Border, and they did have a ridiculous little marriage chapel, complete with a plastic cake for display purposes only. You were prohibited from touching the cake, and they enforced that rule strictly, and diligently.

To be continued...

XLVI

I had to pay 35 dollars because I let her paint her name on the wall of my dorm room. I learned the expensive way that "watercolor" paint doesn't always wash off with just water. I had painted a character from an old cartoon (poorly, I might add), and both had to be painted over by university maintenance to return the walls to their intended eggshell.

Bionca did not approve of Marlee's attempt at art or the spelling of her name and ridiculed the discount graffiti and the way it was so proudly and prominently displayed. Since it was very large and brightly colored, it was constantly on display and Marlee was a perpetual target of Bionca's vitriol and contempt. I don't believe Bionca had ever actually met Marlee, but I firmly believed an introduction would only stoke the fire, so I resided to let Marlee remain an unseen target. It was like firing into the darkness from the porch when a suspicious sound is heard; that's all it was.

I don't know why I complained, it was my overly-generous, always wonderful, always understanding, forever supportive parents who paid for the wall, along with the breadth of my squandered education (though I did learn that thing about watercolor paint). Their empathy for me and my hopeful romanticism made them feel obligated to support even the most gossamer chances of lasting happiness.

They had met Marlee when she and a few friends accompanied me on a trip back home to investigate proof of the legend of hometown thrift stores. I was often wearing the proof of its bounty, but the origin needed to be seen to be believed.

I was eager to see (and feel) Marlee in her new old sweaters and maybe a skirt if she could locate one that fit. It was not impossible to find such things, but I understood optimism usually overtook reality, and that her cart might be left vacant.

The same was never true for me. I had clothes, lots of clothes. The resulting bounty of that day's visit to the thrift store would depend on whatever picture in whatever magazine or whatever character in whatever movie was wearing and defining my current cool. Presently, it was plaid pants, button-up collared short-sleeved shirts, ringer t-shirts, and ties I had no reason to wear, thus, no reason to buy. I didn't golf (except for mini), but I admired and adopted the style of classic golfers. Not contemporary golfers adorned with baseball hats and khakis, although Payne Stewart, a golfer who still played, wore the style of clothing I wanted to own and wear.

A few of the prime finds of this visit so far were: three striped polo shirts that were not full button-ups and would definitely be worn by golfers (or bowlers) several decades before; numerous ties, two pairs of plaid polyester pants (did they make them with another fabric?); and a non-ringer t-shirt that was vaulted into the upper rankings of top finds I had ever discovered! It was an old, weathered t-shirt embellished with an image of Fred Flintstone and his family on the front with a metallic fleck iron-on. This certainly would have been enough to secure entrance in my wardrobe but wait! Then I saw the back. I am very, very rarely stricken speechless by anything, but the only words I could summon were, "Oh...my...God. Oh...my...God. OH MY GOD!" On the back of the shirt, in fuzzy ironed-on letters (awesome) were the words "Grand Poobah" and a giant number 10 (also in fuzzy numbers that had been ironed on).

I was vibrating with joy and had lost any empathy for Marlee or sympathy for the emptiness of her cart. I had unearthed a treasure from the racks of t-shirts announcing the picnics of assorted local companies and, with a thoughtless callousness, wrapped up Marlee and kissed her in between exclamations of glee about forever being known as the Grand Poobah.

I try not to act on poor decisions, thus I do not regret many, if any, of the decisions I act upon. My behavior is intentional, and options are exhaustively considered and accepted, then acted upon or dismissed. I put thought behind them and try to only take action after a good deal of objective consideration. All that being said, on the car ride home, I regretted a decision to pass on an opportunity to buy a t-shirt I just didn't understand. My confusion fueled the decision, and that was regrettable.

"Too Old for Green Bananas" was the announcement declared in jovial, fluorescent text on the black t-shirt. I didn't get it. I'm 18, and I don't consider myself too old for much of anything. High chairs? Yes. Sippy cups? Sure. Diapers? I'm simultaneously too old and not old enough by decades. My lack of understanding resulted in what businesspeople call a "white miss." I think. I don't converse with a whole lot of businesspeople...or golfers, though I like their fashion sense.

I was the perfect age, however, for a puffy, horizontally-s eamed, butterfly-collared jacket with a bull dog patch on the breast and the company name, "Mack." It was my "Mack jacket." It was not the 1970s, and I am not a pimp, but I had a Mack jacket, and I repeatedly referred to it by the name I created.

I liked Marlee quite a bit, maybe even more than the additions to my already impressive attire. I liked her more than the garments I added in her company (maybe not the Grand Poobah shirt or the Mack jacket, but they set the bar unattainably high). The shirt and the jacket would, again, outlast another generation, several more decades, and another relationship.

My wonderful, generous, and caring parents still ask if I've talked to her recently. I never say no, even though I haven't. I only say, "Not recently."

XLVII

Ela had herpes.

She didn't have any diseases, certainly not communicable diseases, when we kissed and spent the night together. It's a shame the phrase "spent the night together" has come to imply intercourse, because there was none of that. In obsolete terms used almost exclusively in middle school locker rooms, on the school bus, or around lunchroom tables, we made it to "second base." To clarify, because everyone's definition of the "base" system varies, we kissed, open-mouthed, and my hands toured her leviathan breasts (over her bra) and shapely form (over her unmentionables). The flesh underneath her unmentionables remained unblemished, untouched, and unpolluted...at least by me.

The guilty party, which I strenuously tried to believe was not her, was a member of the university football team who had been unfaithful with another (probably) innocent victim of another unfaithful football-playing predator.

I had been accused of deifying women I thought highly of and vaulting them to an unsustainable level of righteousness and nobility. They knew they could not fulfill the image I had projected upon them, and I'm not entirely sure they wanted to. It was not who they genuinely were, so it was uncomfortable and probably less fun and carefree by comparison. But being carefree (and fun?) in this instance resulted in a sexually transmitted disease and would warrant a series of uncomfortable discussions for the rest of her life.

We were having one of those uncomfortable conversations right now. Bathed in the muted light that stumbled through the window of my living room, she stared up at me with teary, still-beautiful eyes, and told me all about the series of regrettable decisions that led to her current state. She'd no doubt seen, and ignored, the countless articles and news stories about the tawdry lifestyle promoted by the men on college sports teams. I had read those articles and seen the subsequent features on news programs as a frame of reference, but I believed them to be fact.

Ela was a dancer, and decided she wanted to be a cheerleader too. To her it was a progression, and a natural one, so she tried out and was embraced by the cheerleading team (and more aggressively, the football team members too). My guess—had I been asked, which I wasn't—saw her head filled with the traditional American Dream of a cheerleader dating a football player and wearing the letterman's jacket I didn't know A) existed, B) he wore, or C) he owned if it did exist. It was more probable the origin of their relationship took place in the coatroom or on the beer-stained rug of a house party, but movies and old pop songs ushered me to believe it had grown out of a bonfire on a secluded beach somewhere. Since the city where the university resided was land-locked, I didn't think a secluded beach was a realistic venue. They could have met on a Spring Break outing, but I was fairly certain relationships were not started on those beaches. I believed, and had seen blurry photographic proof, things happened on spring break beaches, but not the incubation of relationship seedlings.

Her cheeks were streaked, and her words were shaky and spilling over with regret as she explained exactly what had happened. It was by no means a spontaneous act, and it was the epitome of carelessness to not ask the questions whose answers would have mandated protective measures. But those questions had not been asked, and those measures, though simple, were not taken, and now she was sentenced to an eternity of teary, embarrassing explanations. In the future, others, maybe others who would not routinely have to worry such worries or fear such fears, would need to approach what they had previously considered a natural, zesty, and impromptu engagement vigilantly and with caution or they, too, would be condemned to explain uncomfortable circumstances to partners who were inexperienced.

I could tell Ela was upset and shaken to her core, which begged two questions she could not adequately answer now, or ever: Why wasn't she more careful, or careful enough? Also, why was she still with him (which she was)? The first question could not be sufficiently answered and being someone who never considered the overconsumption of alcohol an acceptable excuse for careless behavior, there was no acceptable answer. The second answer could understandably exist because it would negate the necessity of these manner of conversations. I was unaware of any heightened strain of "super-herpes" she might potentially contract through continued unprotected intercourse, but if he was unfaithful once without consequences, he could be again, and he might, then she might, succumb to something that even a watery confession wouldn't extinguish.

XLVIII

We were sitting in a circle trading stories about being "poor kids," and Maggie was trying in her adorable, boisterous way to explain she was "the poor kid" by telling us about what passed as toys in her destitute childhood.

She was of diminutive height and often wore elephant-legged jeans that rarely revealed her tiny, cute little sneakers. Her hair was short and announced a pleasant and charismatic greeting when she thrashed her cheeks from side to side.

Maggie was telling us about "the bean machine," which was not a machine at all, even a simple one, but instead a bag of loose, uncooked beans, probably navy, a marker, and the imagination of a child, which was free. Maggie and her siblings were instructed to draw faces on the beans with markers (probably "borrowed" indefinitely from a school, library, or other institution that had insufficient funding, and most likely received them as a donation). Magically, the beans became characters and thus, toys.

The bean machine made a strong contribution to the campaign for being named the poor kid of our circle of friends, but when combined with the admission and explanation of how her and her siblings used to bathe together in a trashcan with a garden hose, no arguments would be strong enough.

She never went into detail, or even mentioned the ridicule and cruelty of the torment she undoubtedly endured when fellow schoolchildren discovered her economic status. They were the same children who were poisoned by the ignorance of not knowing anyone or personally anything outside of their own primetime televised, top 10 box office and top 10 radio charted myopic world. A lack of familiarity led to disdain, which eventually led to jeering, then derision, then hatred from who chose to look elsewhere so they wouldn't have to face their own unsatisfactory lives.

Group bathing in a trashcan?! Maggie had genuine reason for her shine to have been dulled by existence, but she beamed with excitement about and disbelief of everything, all the time. The word "amazing" has come to be overused in our society and diluted as a result. Foods are not sincerely amazing, because every being who has existed since the invention of fire has been able to comprehend ostensibly how it is made. "That dress" is not amazing, and it is not accurate to say the vast majority of the experiences characters on television call "amazing" are, in fact, genuinely astonishing. Maggie was not mentally deficient, or simple in any way, yet she was simultaneously exhilarated and fascinated in the minutia of daily life. It was childlike in its sheer rapture and satisfaction. It was endearing, and a crush quickly enveloped me. I was smitten.

I did not grow up poor in the ways Maggie described, but I did not at all grow up in an environment of opulence, either. My parents both had jobs, and they always saw that my sister and I had food and clothes for school and cold weather, but we were not spoiled, and I doubt they would have spoiled us even if they could afford it.

I worked as a referee for kids' soccer games back in high school, then very briefly at a sandwich shop in my sophomore year at the university. I barback, too, but I still hold the distant dream of being a rock and roll star, a rockabilly star. I already have the hair and the style, and I liked the only gin and tonic I ever had, so it seems to me to be obvious I start a band, too. I even wrote a song both for and about Maggie.

We were close, and she stayed over one night on the bunk bed with the mini-couch underneath. We kissed and held each other, but one of our friends told me she "thought I was so cute and cuddly, like Winnie the Pooh." It was pretty obvious a relationship or any physical advancement was just not in the cards. I know the saying refers to playing cards, not greeting cards, but I imagine if did refer to greeting cards, she would imagine mine covered with glitter and kittens.

When something exhilarated her, which happened almost perpetually, she would yell, "Oh my God!" Realistically, there should be many more exclamation points (think, just pressing down on a keyboard and holding the key). You were alerted of her presence when she was not yet in sight by the announcement of "Oh my God!"

The song wrote itself.

"Oh my God!"
"Oh my God!"
is what she's screamin'
when she's screamin' like a teapot
when it's steamin'
I'd swear that she's
possessed by a demon
when she screams, "Oh my God!"
Oh my God
Oh my God
Oh my God
when she screams, "Oh my God!"
Oh my God,
she wraps her arms around me
then I pick her up
and spin her around me
I think true love has finally found me
when she screams, "Oh my God!"
(chorus)

Then she looks at me
with a little smile
and she grabs me again
'cause it's been a while
if she gives me a chance
I'll stroll her down the aisle
when she screams, "Oh my God!"
when
she
screams,
"OH
MY
GOD!"

L (part 10)

I will readily admit I did not intimately know Violet or how she would be as a partner or wife, nor how our life or marriage would be, nor how the dynamic of our relationship would develop. She was no more an expert than I and had no immediately intimate examples of a successful long-term union but spoke and carried herself as if she did. I generally presented as a passive human, and without a frame of reference, errantly believed a partner, or any reasonable person, would act with gratitude and civility if they usually got their way. I was never married, so it just seemed a pragmatic and respectful means of conducting oneself.

Little did I know this would lead to (or degenerate into) her taking advantage of the situation and escalating to the point of manipulation. I had previously been an affectionate person and enjoyed the attention of those I viewed as attractive. This was not exclusive to physical aesthetics, and I wholeheartedly believed a person's personality and the resulting actions made them more or less attractive. The opinion that intellectual attractiveness did not at all equate to sexual attraction was one Violet did not understand, thus did not agree with.

To Violet, the notion that friendliness and sexual intentions could be independent of each other was foreign and an unacceptable characteristic of married men. In her mind, friendship eventually led to infidelity, a feeling of inferiority, and heartbreak. So, a welcoming of friendly, platonic hugs became declarations of untouchable, sacred personal space, and emotional seclusion. This kept everyone away from me, including, and most importantly, women. She could certainly not say defiantly what all married men did or did not or could or could not do according to (unwritten) laws carved in marble, but she spoke as if what she knew, and spouted, was gospel.

I would often treat her to a complimentary meal at the restaurant and microbrewery when I became a member of the management team, a promotion that came quickly after ownership knew I had just become a "family man." It was assumed this meant my professionalism would restrict me from excessive fraternization with the staff, which was already a personal rule I adhered to in any position of authority, but it meant I wasn't "friends with girls," something Violet vehemently declared married men did not do. These circumstances continued and grew to other management jobs in other states over several years, and other intentionally missed opportunities to bond and eventually, life became lonely.

Appreciation for the free meals and treats was not voiced publicly, nor privately for that matter. Criticism of the free food and beverages, as well as the background music, the level at which it was played, the temperature of the establishment, and anything else detected by scrutinizing, suspicious eyes was proclaimed quite publicly at a volume worthy of explanation and apology, and privately for that matter.

"Those are too short." "You can see your pee-pee in those." "You shouldn't let them wear those." It felt like everything I did or chose, regardless of whether it directly affected her or not, was attacked and denigrated. I knew how I conducted myself at work, what I wore, the environment I oversaw, was applauded by those who supervised me, and held a personal stake in the success of my position. I objectively knew I was good at what I did, and how I did it, but when isolation limited positive comments, and the only reaction to any situation was critical, it was a challenge to feel proud.

The commencement of our marriage had sprinted by without the pragmatic, necessary caution it deserved, and continued running into dangerous territory. Had we dated longer than a day, it could reasonably be stated we would not have been married. But we were absorbed by the romance of it and entranced by the freedom that accompanied it. Personally, and I only became harshly aware of it after the self-reflection isolation allows, I was a young romantic enamored by a beautiful face and bold independence, and I arrogantly believed I could make it work. "It" in this case was an imbalanced, unhealthy marriage, and a permanent decision.

To be continued...

XLVIX

The following is a work of fiction.

"We're gettin' jacked. Hold on."

Timothy had graciously volunteered to give Shirley and me a ride to the charity bicycle ride we were participating in today. It started early (six a.m.), and that was probably because the charity bicycle ride was attempted by those with the disease we were raising money to fight, and some whose only disease was old age and the resulting diminishment of their spryness. Such attendees were slower than those of us who were neither and needed more daylight to ride under.

Shirley was up front in the passenger's seat, and I sat in the back of Timothy's vintage family automobile. He had obviously kept it meticulously clean and as true to the original condition as possible. I don't think cars of that era came standard with the same flamboyance the current rims were exhibiting, but no one could or would argue Timothy had style.

Neither of us had a car or access to one, so we graciously accepted Timothy's offer to drive us to the event. He was a patron of the coffee shop where I worked, and Shirley frequented. He was entertaining and kind, and as modest as someone dancing and singing while he waited for his beverage could be.

Shirley and I were invited to a family and friends gathering at his home earlier that summer. It was a charming oasis in what could be affectionately described by people who lived there as "the ghetto." If you were not a resident of the hamlet, it was universally understood you did not possess the right to use that term without the expectation of recourse. I comprehended how it earned that title based on the streets and neighborhood surrounding it. They were dotted with liquor stores, fast food establishments, check cashing places, and watchmen for unseen (but very present) drug dealers. They were called "hustlers" and they spent their days "hustling." Timothy was protected by a shield of respect brought about by something more than just possessing a nice house and a couch worthy of its plastic covering.

His shield was absent as we ventured downtown at the break of day through a neighborhood coated with broken glass and crumpled, unread newspapers. The sun was reluctantly rising, and the amateur hustlers were interviewing the sparse, early morning occupants of the borough trying to find offerings they could steal, then sell for money they could use to buy the crippling substances to make their reality (briefly) change to a more livable one. Possibilities were thinner than the zombies clutching their arms and uttering threats and grievances to the ghosts surrounding them.

Such a being had approached Timothy's car as he paused at a pointless and hazardously placed stop sign. Timothy quickly held out one arm to restrain Shirley like a well-intentioned, but powerless mother attempting with futility to protect their offspring before stopping suddenly. His other arm was also straightened and extended toward the zombie trying to "jack" his mint-condition sedan.

He held his hand perpendicular to the ground and spread his fingers wide while he uttered something inaudible in the direction of the strung-out character who meant to do him harm. The palm remained open and rigid as the now-wide eyes and mouth attached to the loosely-bolted bones and filthy rags that covered them reacted as if Timothy had tightly grasped the zombie's sleeve in his fist, and violently jerked the face, bones, and dirty clothes against the rigid metal frame of his car. His elbow did not bend or pull a tight fist of zombie with it back and into the car, but a loud, metallic *thud* was followed by the zombie crumpling to the asphalt. A cloak of blood and spittle lowered over the bent, screaming face, and the zombie lay writhing in anguish.

"Let's get out of here," Timothy said as he checked his mirrors and shifted into drive. His tires spun, and their rubber grabbed at dirt and road as he sped away.

"What was that? What did you just do?" I asked, still thawing from the frozen state I was in.

"Nothing. Do you guys want coffee? I know a place downtown."

"Um, I could have an Americano, but what was that? With your hand? Is that guy all right?"

"I'll have a coffee," Shirley pleasantly chimed in.

"Shouldn't we go back? See if he's okay?" I asked.

"No, we're not going back. There were others, and they got his money and drugs, and shoes and coat by now. What could we do for him?"

"I don't know, he was bleeding, and..."

"Here's the place. We'll pop in, and they have Danishes, too, but you probably shouldn't have...maybe you should. Did you eat? Shirley, did you eat?"

Timothy was a good friend and a kind man. I don't know what that was back there, what he did to the guy that was trying to "jack" us, but he's a good man and a good friend.

Timothy was talking to a large man, probably the owner, who just emerged from the door in the floor behind the counter. While they talk, my head is drifting away to thoughts of Shirley in a similar pair of bicycle pants and a weathered, old, now unreadable t-shirt from another fundraiser bicycle ride years ago. These pants had a stripe on them—a bright pink one.

"Did he have red shoes on?" The hulk of a man boomed through his mustache.

"Yes, I think," Timothy responded as he collected the paper cups from the counter and distributed the beverages while we thanked him and put a few dollars in the tip jar.

"Fuckin' Horace! That junkie motherfucker!" The owner apparently knew him and did not hold him in very high regard.

"That fuckin' crackhead will steal the numbers off the god-damn register keys if you turn your back on him! Horace stole the chocolates, tips, even the goddamn biscotti when I turned around to get him a Goddamn free cup of water! I caught him, too, and ran after him, but look at me! I ain't catchin' no skinny little crackhead! Fuckin' guy!"

As he continued his passionate tirade, the cheeks hovering over his mustache became increasingly flushed. My cheeks grew warm too, as I tried to recall every shred of every minutia of every image, smell, and feeling (both physical and emotional) from the evening before, when Shirley invited me to her apartment to watch a movie about gangsters engaging in gangster activities. We only watched, and didn't really watch, what we saw if we opened our eyes while kissing. It played in the background as she rubbed my shoulders and intermittently kissed the back of my neck and head.

As we stood several feet from the mustachioed volcano who looked as though he could pop with every underlined exclamation, I thought only of Shirley's smooth form and how much she had looked (and felt) like someone had held her by the rings of the curls playing over her scalp and dipped her into a liquid, starless night. Her legs were shiny and black, and smooth against my fingertips and palms. This man was seconds and syllables away from erupting, and I had sunk into the thoughts of pressing against Shirley's muscles and the skin-tight Lycra that coated them. I lost myself in the thoughts of how her tongue felt against mine.

As I was about to surrender to the fantasy and oblivion that accompanied it, two police officers entered the coffee shop. The small shop fell silent, even the man behind the counter, and the officers scanned the tiled breadth between the rack of unwholesome, unnatural snacks and the adult magazines. Timothy said nothing and instinctively placed his hands on the counter, shoulder width apart. As the uniformed men examined the peripheries of the establishment, Timothy made small circles with the end of the index finger on his left hand and moved his lips. I heard a low hum, like the motor of a refrigerator, but no words. The officers simultaneously turned and faced each other. They looked as though they were going to kiss, but instead turned and, in unison, said, "Okay" and hastily walked back out the door.

Timothy was unaware I had seen him twirling his finger, and I asked him about it.

"What was that, sir? What...what was that? And thank you again for the beverages, but what is that thing?" Despite taking pride (usually) in my ability to communicate and effectively use language, confusion and curiosity rendered me inept.

"Bring your Americano and let's go!" Timothy said. He might have been blushing as he turned and playfully shimmied out... maybe? I hesitated a step or two, so I could genuinely appreciate the pink stripe clinging to Shirley's thigh. She was a stronger cyclist than I, and although I would have ample opportunities to watch her from behind, I would be more focused on my burning lungs and muscle pain as I did.

L (part 11)

As a diagnostic examination for a degenerative nerve disorder I would soon find out I had, and would continue to have until I transitioned from alive to not, I had to undergo a spinal tap. It was called a "lumbar puncture" in medical terms, but entertaining mockumentaries entitled This Is Lumbar Puncture are not produced, understandably so.

My wife, and partner for over seven years, drove me to the appointment where a large syringe would be inserted directly into my spinal column, and spinal fluid would be extracted for examination. I had never undergone this procedure, and what little I heard about it from those who had made me nervous. I was certain being tense, which I most certainly was leading up to it, was not optimal, though I only became more so as I thought about what needed to happen to me in a successful examination. Mental self-preservation would not allow me to entertain the possibility of an unsuccessful one.

Violet did not speak to me on the trek to the physician's office where the lumbar puncture would be performed. Her silence was a reaction to the "discovery" of the book you are currently reading. She used her superior knowledge of computers and the assistance of spyware to hack into my email and find the few chapters sent to Will, the Best Man at our wedding, and repeated character in several of these chapters. I had never kissed Will on the mouth, but I could do (and have done) worse. Just not my thing.

I was writing this book in secret because I knew there was a better chance of it being accepted, possibly even appreciated, though doubtfully ever endorsed, if I kept it secret until it was finished. I had a strong suspicion her reaction would be consistent (and negative), but even after years of living with her every emotion brought about by a spectrum of experiences, I didn't want to believe I would be alone today.

I was hunched over a paper-covered table, and a tube of stiff stainless steel was manipulated in between my vertebrae, and Violet sat silently watching. She couldn't have known how much a held finger, or the warmth of a touch would have meant. She couldn't have, and still sat in silence as her husband, the man who would do nearly anything to make her life more comfortable and pleasant, lay scared and in pain.

The test was performed skillfully, and Violet remained silent as we returned to the home we owned, the dogs we raised or permanently fostered, and the collections of collections of amusing, but useless pieces of our life. She couldn't have known how much a (gentle) hug would have eased my physical and emotional discomfort, but she would have received a sliver of insight had she been speaking or listening to me.

I opted to endure the discomfort of standing, corralling employees, and dealing with guests because the ache I would suffer at work paled in comparison to the disease I would experience at home with Violet. So, I showered and had a wet towel wrapped around my hips as I wiped the steam from the mirror. I began shaving when I heard the quickening pounding of kettle drums unnecessarily announcing Violet's ascent from downstairs.

She was screaming at me with a guttural bark spawned by a hate and anger and misguided betrayal I have never known and hope not to. Her words fired through the air and embedded themselves in my pink, warm skin. They burnt.

She inexplicably accused me or penning "pornography," entirely ignoring she was my first sexual partner, and could be my only if she was civil and treated me with the respect currently absent in our union.

She also declared that either her or the book was leaving. I knew this was an idle threat like the pornography allegation, but the time to argue my position was not now.

She closed the distance between us and swung the hammered fist on the end of her arm.

Pow!

The room went white and its edges began to leak darkness as I shook my head to restore cognition. I held her by the throat as I pushed her against the wall, and instinctively growled a ridiculous threat I remembered from a movie.

I would never, could never, even in retaliation, strike her. It's not who I am, have ever been, or ever want to be. I felt grotesque for even putting a hand on her neck to protect me from being hit again. It was not effective, and Violet punched me in the face again before I left for work. The second punch was not preceded by screams or threats, nor signals of its inevitability. It felt the same, and I felt the same about it.

I did leave, but it was months later after the grind and squeal of hurt and anger and betrayal had settled before a new storm of emotion could dust up. I had no real friends during my marriage and declared, "I wasn't allowed." This is an inaccurate statement. I knew my marriage was not ideal, and I even knew it was bad, but Violet repeatedly shared her feelings about men and their unreliability, and I was different. I was going to change her mind and show her that a man can be responsible and loyal and good. I am a good man, and good men didn't leave and break promises.

I left when it became clear nothing I did or did not do altered her or her behavior (which had reached its unacceptable apex). I knew it had been bad, but how bad had never been specifically defined. I knew it was not ideal, but I never thought to use the terms boldly on display on the wall of the bathroom hallway under the heading, *Signs You Are in an Abusive Relationship.*

I had to wait in that hallway, and I read down the poster.

1. A Perfect Start At first, many abusive relationships are actually incredibly romantic, but the romantic gestures are usually ploys to captivate you and distract you from what is to come.

2. Picking Up Speed The relationship moves very quickly, but you excuse its intensity because you think its love.

Put-downs

The Guilt Trip

Irrational Jealousy

The list went on and I kept thinking Check. Check. Yep. I remember that day. Yes.

The more I read, the more signs I was in an abusive relationship spawned more memories of more specific instances. My mind's inclination was to be defensive, and deny the realization I actually was, and had been, in an abusive relationship.

I'm not...I'm...Come on...

My objections were hollow against the word in large black letters next to a phone number for a hotline. VICTIM. Its undeniable truth stung and lay heavy in my belly. The excitement of being out with new friends vanished, and my truth and I excused ourselves to go be alone. We stayed in seclusion, in hurt, in regret, in defeat, in a hole of paralyzing depression until one thought pulled me out, dusted me off, and shuffled me off to a new life, a life I wanted and deserved.

The thought was, *you got out.*

La fin.

ABOUT THE AUTHOR

Things I have done: hosted a game show, been a Central Staff member of the Mentor Program at the University of Pittsburgh, hosted the pilot of a talk show (it was one of the ones that became nothin'), founded and ran a baking business*, won Best Cookie in Portland, competed in and completed an Olympic-distance triathlon*, played the title role in an independent movie (I was Jesus and Dracula)*, wrote and published a book (*Ministry of Love*)*, wrote and finished the book you are currently reading, participated in and excelled at improvisational theatre*, assisted in running a play group*, skipped a grade, worked as a promotional model, worked as a nude model (for drawing classes)*, managed a variety of food service establishments (including: a coffee shop, independent restaurants, franchises, multi-unit operations [with a total staff of—150 people], a pizza house, a world famous lobster house, and a microbrewery), painted faces at fairs, refereed children's soccer games, worked at a day shelter for homeless teens*, worked at an overnight shelter for homeless teens*, worked at a residential shelter for homeless and battered women*, endured 18 months of chemotherapy*, been roommates with a movie star, performed stand-up comedy (as my fictitious twin brother)*, had multiple articles published in a music magazine, rode in the MS150 twice (before I was diagnosed with multiple sclerosis), and spoke to physical therapy students about loss and living with a handicap*. I have an admirable wit, a great sense of humor, a positive outlook on life, and a respectable pinball presence. I love pinball, cookies, and love.

*after I was diagnosed with multiple sclerosis